Eyewitness
MARS

Engraving from H. G. Wells's
War of the Worlds

Mars Global Surveyor

Meteorite from Mars

Crater cluster
in Arabia Terra

Mars in the
Noachian Age

Mars Pathfinder

Hipparchus

Eyewitness

MARS

Written by
STUART MURRAY

Editor
EDWARD S. BARNARD

DK

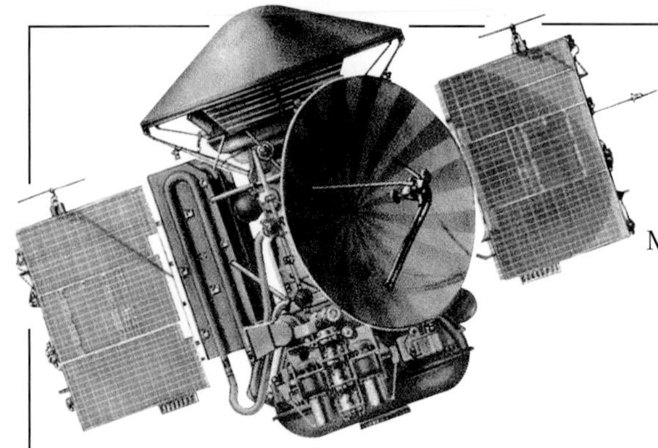

Mars 3 spacecraft

Model of a
Martian snowflake

Topographical map
of Mars

Ice towers on Mars

DK

DK PUBLISHING, INC.
LONDON, NEW YORK,
MELBOURNE, MUNICH, AND DELHI

DK Publishing, Inc.
Project Editor Anja Schmidt
Senior Art Editor Susan St. Louis
Designer Tai Blanche
Art Director Dirk Kaufman
DTP Coordinator Milos Orlovic
Production Manager Chris Avgherinos
Project Director Sharon Lucas
Creative Director Tina Vaughan

Produced for DK Publishing, Inc. by
Media Projects Inc.
Executive Editor Carter Smith
Editor Edward S. Barnard
Managing Editor Aaron R. Murray
Consultant Tony Reichhardt,
of *Smithsonian Air & Space Magazine*
Designer Laura Smyth, Smythtype
Production Manager James Burmester
Picture Researcher Chrissy McIntyre
Copy Editor Kris Christian

Published by the Penguin Group

Penguin Group (USA) Inc.
375 Hudson Street
New York, New York 10014, U.S.A.

Penguin Books Ltd,
80 Strand, London WC2R 0RL, England

Penguin Group (Canada),
10 Alcorn Avenue, Toronto, Ontario, Canada M4V 3B2
(a division of Pearson Penguin Canada Inc.)

Penguin Books Ltd, Registered Offices:
80 Strand, London WC2R 0RL, England

First published by DK Publishing in 2004
03 04 05 06 07 10 9 8 7 6 5 4 3 2 1

Copyright © 2004 DK Publishing, Inc.

A catalog record for this book is available
from the Library of Congress.
A CIP catalogue record for this book is available
from the British Library (UK)

ISBN: 0-7566-0765-5 (Hardcover)
0-7566-0766-3 (Library Binding)
UK ISBN 1 4053 0718 8

Color reproduction by Colourscan, Singapore
Printed in China by Toppan Printing Co.,
(Shenzen) Ltd.

Discover more at
www.dk.com

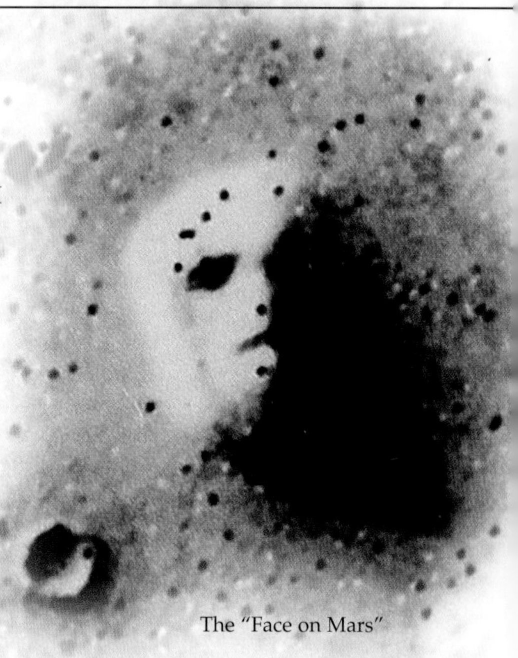

The "Face on Mars"

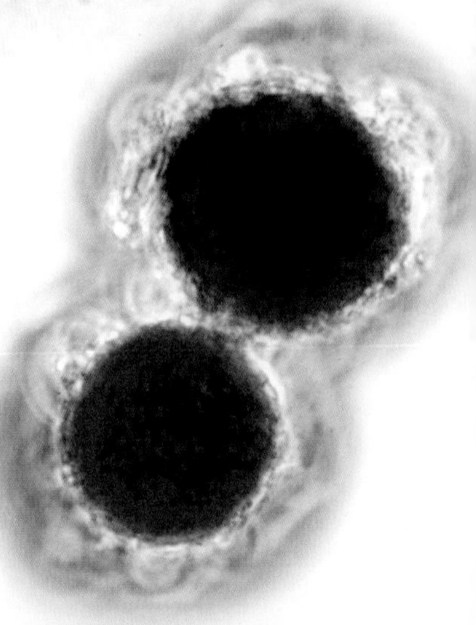

Snow algae

A future Mars rover

Contents

Video camera in tail

Sensors in wings

Spectrometers in nose

Future "Eagle" aircraft

Mars of the ancients

For thousands of years, astronomers had no telescopes. They had only their eyes to observe stars and planets—the "heavenly bodies." Ancient scientists came to know six planets: Mercury, Venus, Earth, Mars, Jupiter, and Saturn. Since they moved past the "fixed" stars of the night sky, the planets earned the name "wandering stars." Four thousand years ago, the Egyptians called Mars—which glows orange-red—*Har Décher*, the "Red One." Centuries later, Babylonians named it *Nirgal*, the "Star of Death." By the 5th century BC, Romans had named the planet Mars, for their god of war. The 2nd-century AD astronomer Claudius Ptolemy believed that Mars, the Sun, Moon, and other planets all revolved around the Earth. Ptolemy's theory was "geocentric"—Earth-centered. This theory ruled the thinking of astronomers for more than 1,400 years.

IN THE NIGHT SKY
Mars, at right, is the second-brightest object in this photograph. Jupiter is the brightest. Planets reflect the strong light of the Sun and do not twinkle like stars, which are trillions of miles farther away. Starlight is distorted—twinkles—in the Earth's atmosphere.

THE PTOLEMAIC SYSTEM
Ptolemy's Earth-centered concept of the Solar System is shown in this 17th-century "celestial planisphere." Seven heavenly bodies revolve around the Earth. From the "geo-center," they are: the Moon, Mercury, Venus, the Sun, Mars (Martis), Jupiter, and Saturn. Colorful planispheres were published in Europe as "celestial cartography," or maps of the heavens.

The first astronomers

Ptolemy gathered ideas about the heavenly bodies from earlier scientists. His great book on astronomy, *The Almagest*, included the teachings of astronomer Hipparchus (190–120 BC), as well as the philosopher Aristotle (384–322 BC). These thinkers understood that the Earth and the heavenly bodies were part of a "cosmos"—an orderly, organized system.

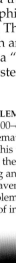

CLAUDIUS PTOLEMY
Ptolemy (c. AD 100–c. AD 170) contributed greatly to mathematics, optics, and geography, and his theories dominated astronomy until the 16th century. He is pictured holding an armillary sphere—a model of the heavens also seen at right near Hipparchus. Ptolemy lived in Alexandria, Egypt, a center of intellectual achievement and learning.

ARISTOTLE
This Greek philosopher divided the cosmos into Earth and Heavens, with the Earth at the center. Heavenly bodies revolved around the Earth. This geocentric system inspired Ptolemy, who built his own theories upon Aristotle's "spherical cosmology."

HIPPARCHUS
Born in Bithynia (now Turkey), Hipparchus was one of the greatest astronomers of all time. He was extremely accurate in his research, charting as many as 1,000 stars and also planets. He developed mathematical methods for finding geographic locations by measuring the positions of stars. This system made navigation at sea possible.

God of war and battle

The ancient Romans worshiped Mars as the divine protector of their empire. He was also the father of Romulus and Remus, the mythological founders of the city of Rome. Mars was second in importance only to Jupiter, the chief Roman god. Mars inspired the name for the month of March, when Roman armies traditionally began their military campaigns. "Martial" is a term for being warlike.

MARS IN ARMOR
Rome was a great empire in the 4th century AD, when this bronze statue of Mars was cast, showing him in body armor. Mars was guardian of the emperor as well as the leading military god worshiped by Rome's legions.

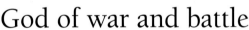

She-wolf

Romulus and Remus

ROMULUS AND REMUS
Mars had twin sons, Romulus and Remus, whose mother was a princess. The babies almost died, but were nursed by a wolf—a creature sacred to Mars. The twins built Rome on the place where they were rescued.

MINERAL OF PROTECTION
Iron oxide hematite, shown above, and iron were symbols of Mars in ancient Rome. Soldiers believed that amulets made of these minerals offered magical protection in battle.

MARS COIN
The profile of Mars in a legionnaire's helmet decorates this coin of the Roman Empire. In early Rome, Mars was also the protector of crops and herds, and farmers called him Silvanus.

Astronomers focus on Mars

THE TERM ASTRONOMY combines the Greek *astron*, "star," and *nomos*, "law." Generally, astronomy is the study of planets and stars and the laws that govern their movements and dimensions. Early astronomers calculated the orbits of heavenly bodies by using mathematics, especially geometry. Poland's Nicolaus Copernicus (1473–1543) led the way to understanding the "heliocentric"— "sun-centered"—theory of the Solar System. This broke with the geocentric system of Ptolemy, which placed the Earth at the center. Later astronomers confirmed Copernicus's theory by using the "perspicillum," or "optick tube." This magnifying device, renamed the telescope, came into use in the 1600s. By the 1800s, scientists studied Mars with increasingly powerful telescopes, and believed they saw canals and seas. Some thought Mars might have age-old civilizations that were further advanced than those of Earth.

NICOLAUS COPERNICUS
This 16th-century Polish astronomer's theory that the planets revolve around the Sun won a growing following among scientists. Leading astronomers such as Johannes Kepler accepted heliocentrism, but many philosophers and religious leaders did not. They believed in geocentrism well into the 1700s.

KEPLER'S ORBITAL MATH
Johannes Kepler (1571–1630) studied mathematics in his native Germany. He was also interested in astronomy. By closely observing Mars, Kepler discovered that the planets follow elliptical orbits, not perfect circles. Using his knowledge of mathematics, he calculated the planets' orbits. Kepler also invented an improved telescope.

HUYGENS AND THE HOURGLASS SEA
Dutch astronomer Christiaan Huygens (1629–1695) was one of those astronomers using ever-improving telescopes to study Mars.

Huygens sketched pictures of a dark smudge he noted on the planet. This was named the Hourglass Sea because of its shape. Seen more clearly in improved telescopes two centuries later, it would be renamed Syrtis Major.

Pondering life on Mars

As a young man William Herschel (1738–1822) moved to England from his native Germany and taught music. Herschel was also a dedicated astronomer who built his own telescopes. He was especially captivated by Mars, which he thought was much like Earth. Huygens and Herschel were among the first to say Mars might have living beings.

William Herschel

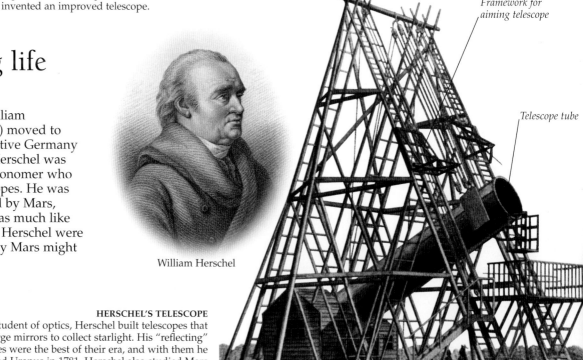

Framework for aiming telescope

Telescope tube

HERSCHEL'S TELESCOPE
A student of optics, Herschel built telescopes that used large mirrors to collect starlight. His "reflecting" telescopes were the best of their era, and with them he discovered Uranus in 1781. Herschel also studied Mars and was convinced that the polar regions of Mars contained areas of ice, which decreased when they partially melted in summer and grew larger in winter.

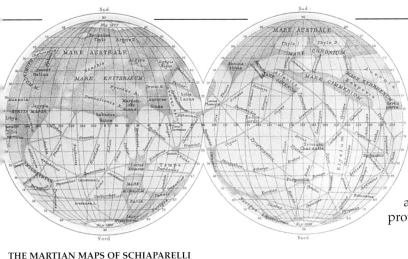

Canal theories

Late in the 19th century, astronomers studying Mars argued bitterly about what they saw in their telescopes. Amateur astronomer Percival Lowell declared there were canals on Mars built by "intelligent beings." Other observers also saw vast, blue Martian seas. Using one of the most powerful telescopes of the day, leading American astronomer Edward E. Barnard found no canals or seas on Mars. He did, however, see high mountains and great plateaus. Scientific research has since proven Barnard was right.

THE MARTIAN MAPS OF SCHIAPARELLI
When he began studying Mars in 1877, Giovanni Schiaparelli (1835–1910) was director of the observatory in Milan, Italy. Schiaparelli was convinced he could see waterways—*canali*, in Italian. He drew maps of what he saw, persuading many astronomers there were canals on Mars.

SCHIAPARELLI'S NAMES
Committed to mapping Mars completely, Schiaparelli worked long nights at his telescope. He labeled the regions and natural features, using Latin and Greek names. Some were from *The Odyssey* and Herodotus, and some were from the Bible. Schiaparelli's names became accepted by future Mars astronomers.

Lowell believed this was water ice

Dark areas: possible vegetation

Lines in Lowell's map show where he believed he saw Martian canals

EDWARD E. BARNARD
A pioneer in celestial photography, American Edward E. Barnard (1857–1923) was the leading observational astronomer of his time. Using the great 36-inch (91 cm) telescope at California's Lick Observatory in 1894, Barnard studied Mars. He was convinced there were no canals— neither natural ones nor canals constructed by Martian beings.

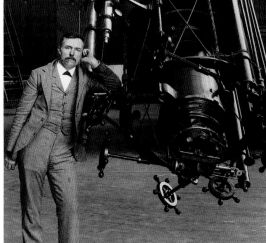

LOWELL'S OBSERVATORY
American Percival Lowell (1855–1916), pictured in 1900, studies Mars at the superb observatory he built in Flagstaff, Arizona. Lowell believed Mars was much like Earth, with water, vegetation, and an atmosphere that humans could breathe. He drew maps, above right, of Martian canals.

Mars and popular culture

No OTHER PLANET excites the imagination of Earthlings like Mars. In the late 19th century, writers began picturing what Martian "intelligent life" could be like. Usually, it seemed hostile. British novelist H. G. Wells first introduced spooky invaders from Mars in his 1897 *War of the Worlds.* Wells's story was a best seller that sparked the public's interest in fantastic Martian tales. Since the early movies of the 1920s, audiences have enjoyed Mars adventures that ranged from the creepy to the silly. One of the most terrifying was a 1938 radio broadcast of *War of the Worlds* that sounded like an actual news report of a Martian invasion. From "Flash Gordon" radio programs to the latest feature films, vast audiences have been entertained by Mars in popular culture.

THE MARTIAN CHRONICLES
Science fiction author Ray Bradbury turned the tables with his 1951 *Martian Chronicles,* in which humans invade Mars. There, humans are the alien life-form. They are colonizers who must build new homes in completely strange surroundings.

Martian war machine from the book *War of the Worlds*

H. G. Wells

War of the Worlds

Starting in 1897 with the chilling *War of the Worlds* by H. G. Wells, fiction shaped popular thinking about "Martians." Radio dramatizations also appealed to audiences. In 1938, Orson Welles produced a radio version of *War of the Worlds* that created a sensation that would be remembered for generations to come. Stories like this continued to be popular in 21st-century fiction, radio, film, and television. The latest science fiction stories are rich in scientific and technical descriptions that appeal to modern readers.

RADIO INVASION
Director Orson Welles frightened listeners in 1938 with a realistic broadcast of "War of the Worlds." Welles made it seem as if hostile Martians had landed in New Jersey. Many people panicked and fled their homes, trying to escape what they thought was a Martian invasion.

BRING 'EM ON!
An elderly citizen watches for the Martian invaders announced by Welles's 1938 radio broadcast. Public fascination with science-fiction adventure was fueled by this radio show. Weekly dramas about space hero Flash Gordon attracted millions of radio fans in the 1930s and 1940s

A PRINCESS OF MARS
By Edgar Rice Burroughs
Author of the "TARZAN" Romances

EDGAR RICE BURROUGHS SENDS A SOLDIER TO MARS
Best known as creator of "Tarzan of the Apes," Edgar Rice Burroughs also wrote science fiction. His series of 11 Mars novels, *The Martian Tales,* follow the adventures of Civil War veteran John Carter, who is transported to Mars. There he overcomes dangerous situations, marries, has children, and becomes an important political leader. The book at left is the first in the series.

FLASH GORDON IN COMBAT
In the 1930s, radio spaceman Flash Gordon moved to film to defeat Martian villain "Ming the Merciless" and his spear-carrying fighters (above). Russia had already put Martians in the movies with the 1924 silent film, *Aelita: Queen of Mars.* Later films, such as America's *Mission to Mars* in 2000, were about heroic fictional astronauts.

MARS ATTACKS!
One zany but violent feature film in the Martian-invasion genre was the 1996 *Mars Attacks!* Earthlings must fight and defeat google-eyed and evil Martians who are determined to enslave humanity. As usual with such movies, the Earthlings win.

Ming the Merciless, from the film *Flash Gordon*

MARS IN AN ARTIST'S IMAGINATION
This is an impression of how people in the early 20th century might have thought of Mars. Water-filled canals lead to and from Martian cities where vegetation lines the canals. These green Martians not only have flying machines, but also have their own wings.

On the eve of the Space Age

In the mid-20th century, science fiction about Mars was overtaken by scientific fact. Fast-developing technology gave scientists powerful telescopes, and new electronics offered long-distance communication at the speed of light. The study of light itself, "spectroscopy", made it possible to analyse Martian minerals and the atmosphere. By the 1950s, average temperatures on Mars were found to be far colder than previously thought, and the air much thinner. Past reports of canals on Mars were considered by many astronomers as "optical illusions" caused by inferior telescopes. Some questioned whether vegetation could grow on the planet. Still, imaginative artists pictured Mars with water and greenery, where human colonists could survive and work. The truth about Mars was close at hand, however, as rocket scientists prepared spacecraft to blast off into the Space Age.

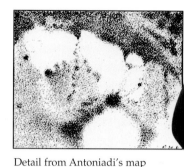

Detail from Antoniadi's map

GERARD KUIPER (1905–1973)
A leading 20th-century astronomer, the Dutch-born Kuiper worked in America most of his career. In 1947, he established that Martian air contains carbon dioxide. Later research would prove carbon dioxide makes up 95 per cent of the atmosphere.

EUGÉNE ANTONIADI (1870–1944)
This Turkish-born French astronomer was at first convinced Mars had canals. Then, in 1909, he studied the planet through the 83-cm (33-in) telescope at Meudon Observatory near Paris – Europe's largest telescope. His maps of Mars showed streaks and chessboard patterns, but no canals.

Carbon dioxide is made up of 1 carbon atom and 2 oxygen atoms

Earth's atmospheric shimmering blurs image

Geological details unclear

PALOMAR OBSERVATORY
In 1948, the world's largest astronomical telescope was dedicated in a new observatory on Mount Palomar in California. A triumph of optics and engineering, the telescope took 20 years to design and construct. It has a 508-cm- (200-in-) wide mirror mounted in a rotating dome.

MARS COMES CLOSER
Palomar's telescope revealed more about Mars than ever before. Yet, as seen in this photograph taken under ideal observational conditions, images were blurred by the Earth's shimmering atmosphere. Astronomers longed to view the heavens from as high above Earth's atmosphere as they could get.

WERNHER VON BRAUN (1912–1977)
U.S. space-flight programs were directed by Wernher von Braun, a former German military rocket designer. Von Braun and other German scientists came to America after World War II to work in the space program. In 1960, Von Braun became the first director of NASA's Marshall Space Flight Center in Alabama. During his 10 years as director, the first manned mission to the Moon took place.

Model based on the V-2 rocket of World War II

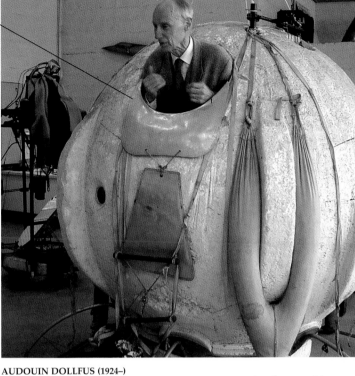

Gondola for passengers

AUDOUIN DOLLFUS (1924–)
To reduce atmospheric interference, French astronomer Audouin Dollfus went up in balloons in the 1950s and 1960s. From six miles (10 km) high, Dollfus used scientific instruments to study Mars, finding the planet had very little water. After 1958, the new National Air and Space Administration (NASA) began launching satellites that carried cameras and scientific instruments.

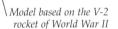

Chesley Bonestell

Chesley Bonestell's Mars

Before his friendship with Wernher von Braun inspired him to visualize Mars in colorful paintings, Chesley Bonestell was both an architect and a motion-picture designer. Bonestell's passion for science fiction was expressed in sets for space-adventure movies. His illustrations of Martian vistas with astronaut colonizers were imaginary, but they stimulated many young people to take an interest in space exploration and astronomy.

A VISION OF MARS
To create this scene, "The Exploration of Mars," Bonestell discussed the latest rockets and equipment with Wernher von Braun. Von Braun's writings on flying to Mars inspired younger scientists as well as painter Bonestell.

The Red Planet revealed

THE UNITED STATES LAUNCHED its first satellites in 1958, racing with the Soviets to be the first to explore the Solar System. In 1962, the National Air and Space Administration (NASA) aimed the probes Mariner 1 and 2 at Venus. Only the second probe succeeded, flashing back photographs of that hot and clouded planet. Mars was next, with two Mariner probes lifting off in November 1964. Mariner 3 failed, but Mariner 4 reached Mars in July 1965, taking 22 photographs from 6,120 miles (9,800 km) away. Scientists and the public were surprised to see a scarred landscape pocked by impact craters. Mars seemed desolate, with no sign of life. In 1969, Mariner missions 6 and 7 sent back many more images, but all were of a Mars that was dry, cold, and dusty.

PRESIDENT JOHNSON
President Lyndon Johnson, right, accepts Mariner probe photographs in January 1964. Presenting the images is Dr. William H. Pickering, director of NASA's Jet Propulsion Laboratory, which designed the Mariners.

Protective shroud covers spacecraft during launch

Atlas rocket boosters powered by liquid oxygen and kerosene

ROCKY AND DRY
Mariner 4 was the first spacecraft to take close-up pictures of Mars. The probe's television camera revealed a crater-scarred, barren landscape.

MARINER 1 LAUNCH
The first of nine probes in the Mariner program lifts off in July 1962. The launch failed, and Mariner 1 was blown up. Mariner 3, the first probe launched toward Mars, also failed. Its protective shroud did not open, which blocked the solar panels, so Mariner 3 died from lack of power.

POCKED WITH CRATERS
Mariner 4's photographic images scanned one percent of the planet's surface. Here, the rugged uplands southwest of the Tharsis region are peppered with impact craters.

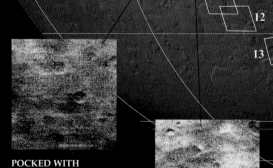

CRATER WASTELAND
The southern hemisphere h more craters. NASA's hope for signs of water turned in a "wasteland of craters."

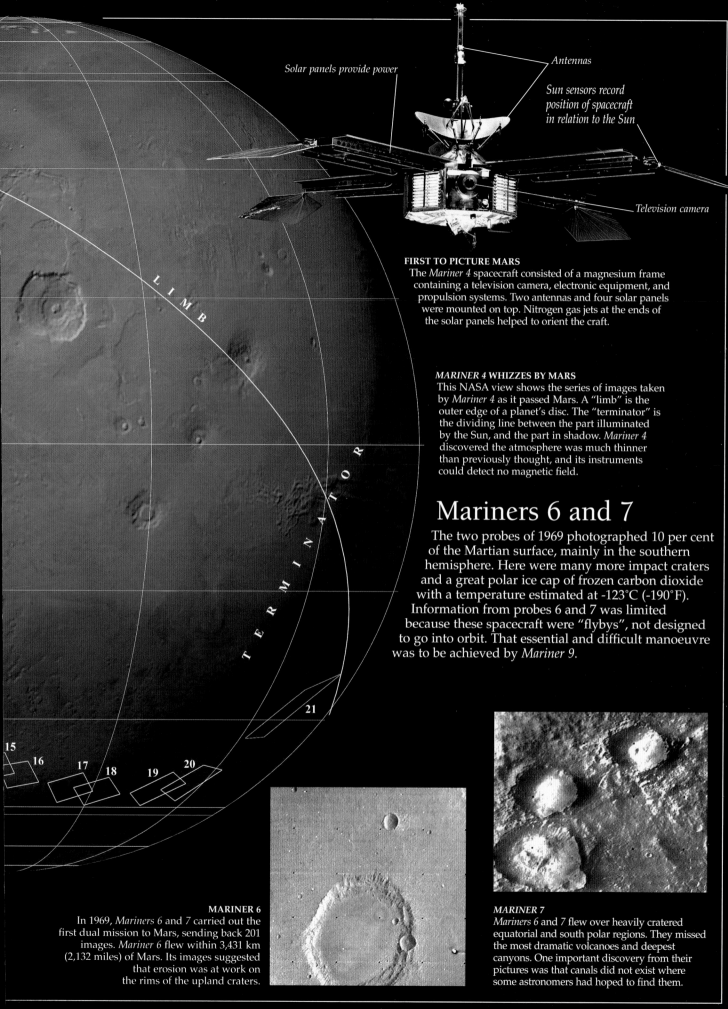

Solar panels provide power

Antennas

Sun sensors record
position of spacecraft
in relation to the Sun

Television camera

FIRST TO PICTURE MARS
The *Mariner 4* spacecraft consisted of a magnesium frame
containing a television camera, electronic equipment, and
propulsion systems. Two antennas and four solar panels
were mounted on top. Nitrogen gas jets at the ends of
the solar panels helped to orient the craft.

***MARINER 4* WHIZZES BY MARS**
This NASA view shows the series of images taken
by *Mariner 4* as it passed Mars. A "limb" is the
outer edge of a planet's disc. The "terminator" is
the dividing line between the part illuminated
by the Sun, and the part in shadow. *Mariner 4*
discovered the atmosphere was much thinner
than previously thought, and its instruments
could detect no magnetic field.

Mariners 6 and 7

The two probes of 1969 photographed 10 per cent
of the Martian surface, mainly in the southern
hemisphere. Here were many more impact craters
and a great polar ice cap of frozen carbon dioxide
with a temperature estimated at -123°C (-190°F).
Information from probes 6 and 7 was limited
because these spacecraft were "flybys", not designed
to go into orbit. That essential and difficult manoeuvre
was to be achieved by *Mariner 9*.

L I M B

T E R M I N A T O R

21

15

16

17

18

19

20

MARINER 6
In 1969, *Mariners 6* and *7* carried out the
first dual mission to Mars, sending back 201
images. *Mariner 6* flew within 3,431 km
(2,132 miles) of Mars. Its images suggested
that erosion was at work on
the rims of the upland craters.

MARINER 7
Mariners 6 and *7* flew over heavily cratered
equatorial and south polar regions. They missed
the most dramatic volcanoes and deepest
canyons. One important discovery from their
pictures was that canals did not exist where
some astronomers had hoped to find them.

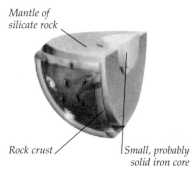

Mantle of silicate rock

Rock crust

Small, probably solid iron core

COMPOSITION OF MARS
Like Earth, Mars is covered by an outer crust. Mars may have frozen water-ice below the crust's surface. Next is the solid, rock-hard mantle, composed of silicate. The core of the planet is made of an iron-rich material that is denser than the mantle.

Mars in the Solar System

THE HEART OF OUR SOLAR SYSTEM is the Sun, a star also known as "Sol." The fiery Sun is the greatest body in the Solar System, 110 times larger than Earth, 200 times larger than Mars. The gravity, or attraction-power, of the Sun controls the movements of nine major planets—the term for bodies that orbit around a star. There are also thousands of smaller bodies in the Solar System, all orbiting the Sun. These include asteroids, comets, and meteoroids. In order, the four planets nearest the Sun, the "inner planets," are Mercury, Venus, Earth, and Mars. Next comes the Asteroid Belt, a great ring of small "planetoids" of varying sizes. The fifth planet is Jupiter, the largest, followed by Saturn, second largest, then come Uranus, Neptune, and Pluto, the smallest planet.

Mars is rocky and cratered

Light areas are covered with dust

Dark areas could be exposed rock

Vital Statistics	
Diameter	4,220 miles (6,794 km)
Average distance from Sun	141.6 million miles (227.9 million km)
Orbital speed around Sun	15 miles/sec (24.1 km/sec)
Sunrise to sunrise	24 hours, 39 minutes (a solar day)
Mass (Earth = 1)	0.11
Volume (Earth = 1)	0.15
Average density (water = 1)	3.93
Surface gravity (Earth = 1)	0.38
Average surface temperature	-81.4°F (-63°C)
Number of moons	2

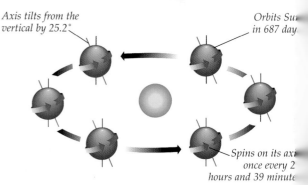

Axis tilts from the vertical by 25.2°

Orbits Sun in 687 days

Spins on its axis once every 24 hours and 39 minutes

AXIS AND ROTATION
Mars spins on an axis tilted about 25 degrees, rotating counterclockwise. One rotation is a Martian day, called a "sol." One sol is 24 hours and 39 minutes. A Martian year has 669 sols.

"FOURTH ROCK" FROM THE SUN
The four worlds nearest the Sun are termed "terrestrial" planets because they resemble Earth. Mars is one and a half times farther than the Earth from the Sun. Though much colder and drier, and lacking breathable oxygen, Mars is the planet most like Earth.

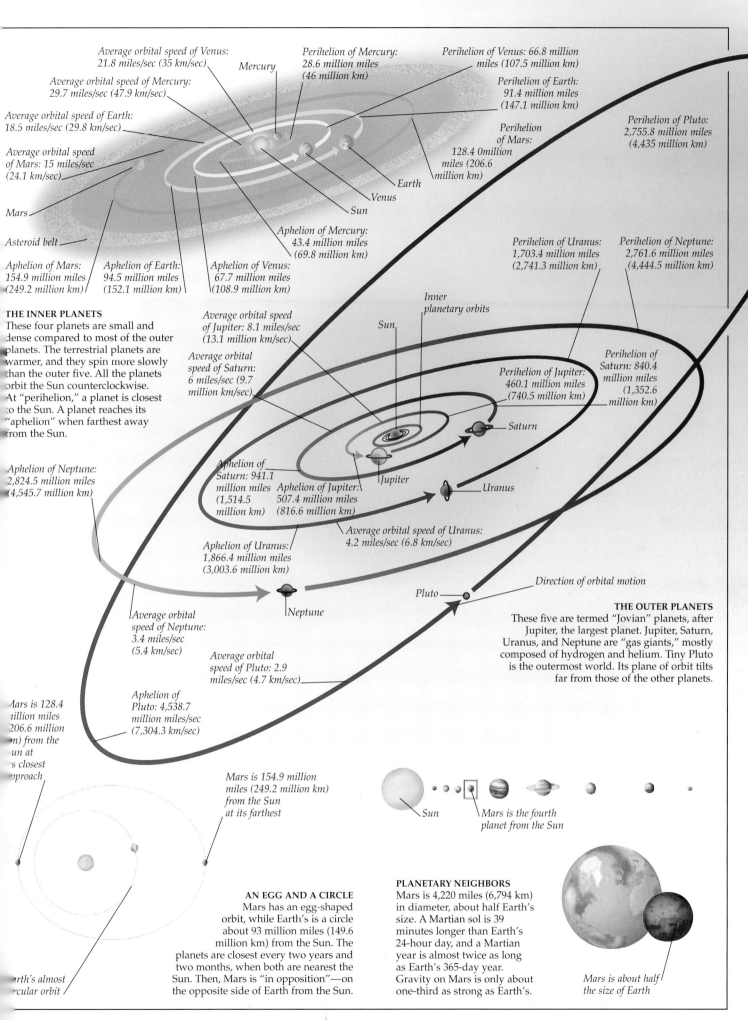

Average orbital speed of Venus: 21.8 miles/sec (35 km/sec)

Average orbital speed of Mercury: 29.7 miles/sec (47.9 km/sec)

Average orbital speed of Earth: 18.5 miles/sec (29.8 km/sec)

Average orbital speed of Mars: 15 miles/sec (24.1 km/sec)

Mars

Asteroid belt

Aphelion of Mars: 154.9 million miles (249.2 million km)

Aphelion of Earth: 94.5 million miles (152.1 million km)

Aphelion of Venus: 67.7 million miles (108.9 million km)

Mercury

Perihelion of Mercury: 28.6 million miles (46 million km)

Perihelion of Venus: 66.8 million miles (107.5 million km)

Perihelion of Earth: 91.4 million miles (147.1 million km)

Perihelion of Mars: 128.4 0million miles (206.6 million km)

Perihelion of Pluto: 2,755.8 million miles (4,435 million km)

Earth

Venus

Sun

Aphelion of Mercury: 43.4 million miles (69.8 million km)

Perihelion of Uranus: 1,703.4 million miles (2,741.3 million km)

Perihelion of Neptune: 2,761.6 million miles (4,444.5 million km)

THE INNER PLANETS

These four planets are small and dense compared to most of the outer planets. The terrestrial planets are warmer, and they spin more slowly than the outer five. All the planets orbit the Sun counterclockwise. At "perihelion," a planet is closest to the Sun. A planet reaches its "aphelion" when farthest away from the Sun.

Average orbital speed of Jupiter: 8.1 miles/sec (13.1 million km/sec)

Average orbital speed of Saturn: 6 miles/sec (9.7 million km/sec)

Inner planetary orbits

Sun

Perihelion of Jupiter: 460.1 million miles (740.5 million km)

Perihelion of Saturn: 840.4 million miles (1,352.6 million km)

Saturn

Aphelion of Neptune: 2,824.5 million miles (4,545.7 million km)

Aphelion of Saturn: 941.1 million miles (1,514.5 million km)

Aphelion of Jupiter: 507.4 million miles (816.6 million km)

Jupiter

Uranus

Average orbital speed of Uranus: 4.2 miles/sec (6.8 km/sec)

Aphelion of Uranus: 1,866.4 million miles (3,003.6 million km)

Average orbital speed of Neptune: 3.4 miles/sec (5.4 km/sec)

Average orbital speed of Pluto: 2.9 miles/sec (4.7 km/sec)

Aphelion of Pluto: 4,538.7 million miles/sec (7,304.3 km/sec)

Neptune

Pluto

Direction of orbital motion

THE OUTER PLANETS

These five are termed "Jovian" planets, after Jupiter, the largest planet. Jupiter, Saturn, Uranus, and Neptune are "gas giants," mostly composed of hydrogen and helium. Tiny Pluto is the outermost world. Its plane of orbit tilts far from those of the other planets.

Mars is 128.4 million miles 206.6 million km) from the un at s closest pproach

Mars is 154.9 million miles (249.2 million km) from the Sun at its farthest

rth's almost rcular orbit

Sun

Mars is the fourth planet from the Sun

AN EGG AND A CIRCLE

Mars has an egg-shaped orbit, while Earth's is a circle about 93 million miles (149.6 million km) from the Sun. The planets are closest every two years and two months, when both are nearest the Sun. Then, Mars is "in opposition"—on the opposite side of Earth from the Sun.

PLANETARY NEIGHBORS

Mars is 4,220 miles (6,794 km) in diameter, about half Earth's size. A Martian sol is 39 minutes longer than Earth's 24-hour day, and a Martian year is almost twice as long as Earth's 365-day year. Gravity on Mars is only about one-third as strong as Earth's.

Mars is about half the size of Earth

Mariner 9: first to orbit Mars

IN EARLY 1971, U.S. AND SOVIET SCIENTISTS hurried to be the first to put a spacecraft into orbit around Mars. Each nation prepared more than one vehicle for this important mission. There were two Mariners and three Soviet probes. The first to launch was Mariner 8, which took off on May 8, but crashed into the Atlantic. On May 30, Mariner 9 blasted off successfully. The first Soviet probe also failed, but the other two soon were racing to Mars. The American vehicle got there first, going into orbit on November 13, two weeks before the Soviets. Mariner 9 did spectacular work, sending back detailed spectroscopic data and 7,300 photographic images that covered the entire Martian surface. Now, Mars could be studied as never before.

High point about 11,300 miles (18,306 km)

12-hour orbit

Deimos

Mars

Phobos

Low point about 800 miles (1,296 km)

MAN-MADE SATELLITE
Mariner 9 was the first artific satellite to orbit Mars, but the planet also has two small moons, Phobos and Deimos. In October 1972, after the fue supply for its controls was us up, the spacecraft was turned off. Scientists expected it to remain in orbit for 50 years before crashing onto the planet's surface.

INTRODUCTION TO PHOBOS
Mariner 9 provided the first close views of Phobos, the larger of Mars's two moons. This image was taken from a distance of 3,600 miles (5,760 km). It shows the cratered surface, with some craters as small as 330 yards (300 m) across.

MARS UNDER DUST
A gigantic dust storm blanketed Mars when Mariner 9 arrived. In this photo, only two of the peaks of the Tharsis volcanoes are visible. Mariner's instruments were shut down to conserve power. The Soviet orbiters sent down landers that failed, and the orbiters ran out of power before the dust cleared.

Volcanoes are the only features visible above dust storm

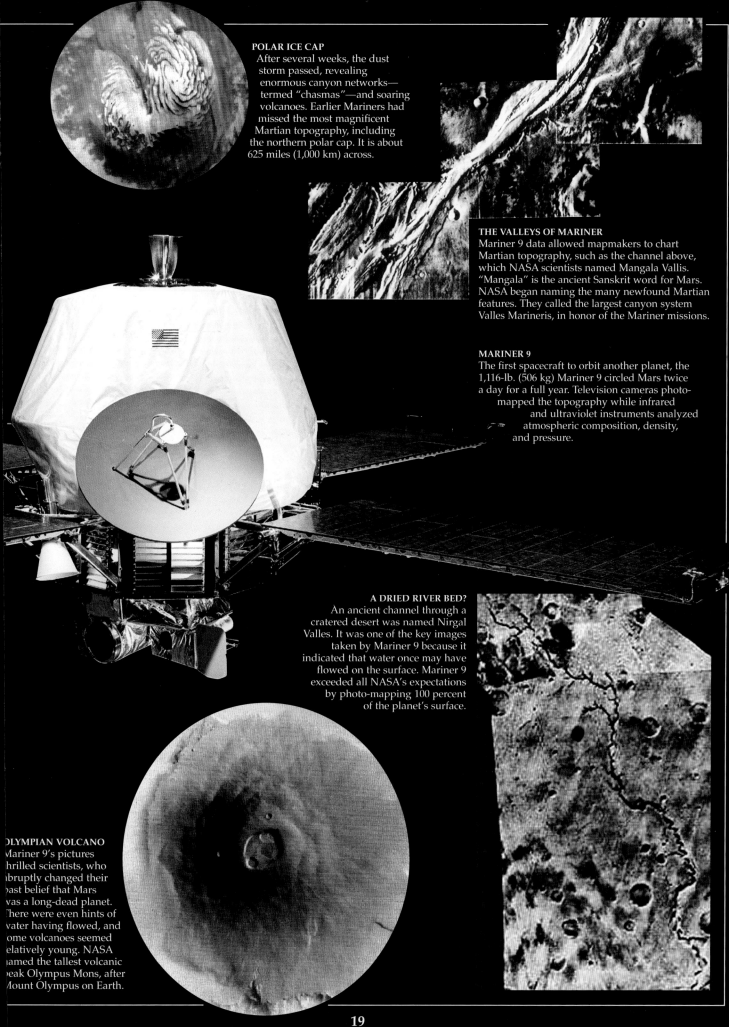

POLAR ICE CAP
After several weeks, the dust storm passed, revealing enormous canyon networks— termed "chasmas"—and soaring volcanoes. Earlier Mariners had missed the most magnificent Martian topography, including the northern polar cap. It is about 625 miles (1,000 km) across.

THE VALLEYS OF MARINER
Mariner 9 data allowed mapmakers to chart Martian topography, such as the channel above, which NASA scientists named Mangala Vallis. "Mangala" is the ancient Sanskrit word for Mars. NASA began naming the many newfound Martian features. They called the largest canyon system Valles Marineris, in honor of the Mariner missions.

MARINER 9
The first spacecraft to orbit another planet, the 1,116-lb. (506 kg) Mariner 9 circled Mars twice a day for a full year. Television cameras photo-mapped the topography while infrared and ultraviolet instruments analyzed atmospheric composition, density, and pressure.

A DRIED RIVER BED?
An ancient channel through a cratered desert was named Nirgal Valles. It was one of the key images taken by Mariner 9 because it indicated that water once may have flowed on the surface. Mariner 9 exceeded all NASA's expectations by photo-mapping 100 percent of the planet's surface.

OLYMPIAN VOLCANO
Mariner 9's pictures thrilled scientists, who abruptly changed their past belief that Mars was a long-dead planet. There were even hints of water having flowed, and some volcanoes seemed relatively young. NASA named the tallest volcanic peak Olympus Mons, after Mount Olympus on Earth.

The first successful landings

IN MID-1975, THE KENNEDY SPACE CENTER in Florida sent Vikings 1 and 2 on their way to Mars. Each carried a lander to be placed on the surface. Launched in August, Viking 1 went into orbit around Mars in June 1976, and in July its lander module descended by parachute onto a boulder-covered northern plain. There, it began searching the soil for signs of life—the mission's main task. In September 1976, Viking 2 put down its lander on a plain halfway around the globe and farther north. The landers took dramatic photographs of the Martian surface and also tested the gases in the atmosphere. Their journeys, successful landings, and the wealth of data they gathered made Vikings 1 and 2 immense triumphs for NASA. Yet, their most important mission had disappointing results: they found no Martian life.

EARTH TO MARS
This dish antenna at a tracking station in Goldstone, California, communicated with the two Viking spacecraft. NASA's Deep Space Network managed this station and two others, in Spain and Australia. Each station had three antennas, with the largest 230 feet (70 m) in diameter.

VIKING PARACHUTES TO MARS
On July 20, 1976, computers on board Viking 1 separated orbiter and lander, and the lander's flight path bent gradually down to Mars. As the descent through the final mile (1.6 km) started, a parachute deployed—as is shown in this illustration. The lander was still in its protective aeroshell.

APPROACHING TOUCHDOWN
This painting shows a key moment soon after the lander's parachute opened. The protective aeroshell has just ejected, and the landing legs have opened up. In about 50 seconds retrorockets fired, slowing down the descent, which ended a minute later with a gentle jolt on Chryse Planitia. Viking 1 was the first spacecraft ever to make a successful landing on another planet.

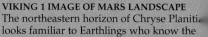

VIKING 1 IMAGE OF MARS LANDSCAPE
The northeastern horizon of Chryse Planitia looks familiar to Earthlings who know the rocky deserts of the American Southwest. Yet, Mars is more barren than any Earthly desertscape, and its sky is rusty-pink from suspended dust. The large boulder, nicknamed "Big Joe," is about 10 feet (3 m) wide and 3 feet (1 m) high.

Biology tests of Martian soil

Mechanical arms on the Viking landers collected soil samples and mixed them with water and life-supporting chemicals. Sensitive instruments checked the mixtures, looking for signs of life such as gas molecules given off by microscopic bacteria. The dusty Martian soils proved sterile, however. Since winds mixed dust from all over the planet, most scientists believed these negative results would be the same everywhere on Mars.

A LANDER'S LABORATORY
Each Viking lander had an onboard laboratory to test soil samples. One instrument fed a sample with nutrients and tried to detect gases normally produced by living organisms. None were found. Another test was for plantlike cells. Soil was heated, and a bright light encouraged cells to grow, but without success.

Nutrient supply

Gas analyzer

Helium gas

Martian soil wetted with nutrient solution

Bright lamp promoted growth of any plant cells for five days

Gases from soil sample separated

Heat broke down any organic chemicals in the soil and converted them into gas

Gas analyzer

VIKING LANDERS
The Viking 1 and 2 landers were the first spacecraft to conduct long-term research on another planet. Each lander had a robotic arm that scooped up soil samples for testing. There were also two rotating television cameras and instruments to study Martian weather. The landers operated until 1982, transmitting 1,400 images to Earth.

Dish antenna

Cameras

Meteorology instruments

Robotic arm and scoop

Robotic arm's scoop

DIGGING IN THE DIRT
The Viking lander's robotic trenching arm with its sharp scoop is tested on Earth before the mission's two launches. The first experiments on Martian soil samples suggested the presence of life, but later review of the results found there was no life. The lander's meteorology instruments are contained in the other extended arm.

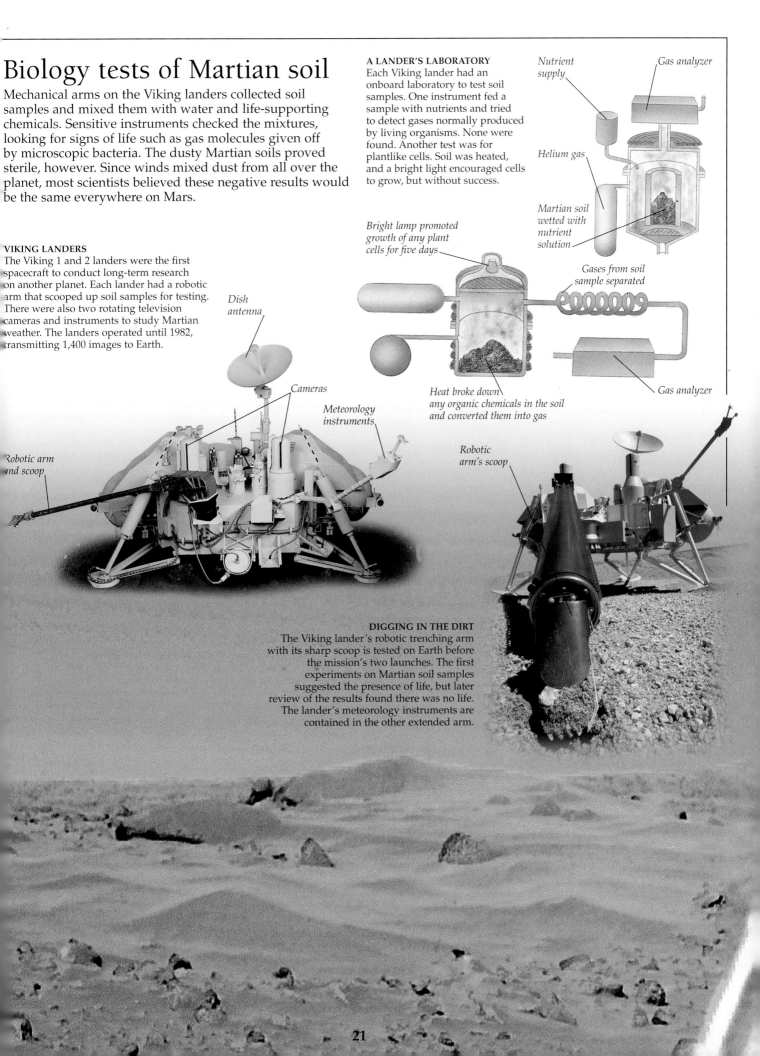

Three ages of Mars

SCIENTISTS BELIEVE MARS has had three major ages, or time periods, each lasting many millions of years. These ages are named for different geographic areas of Mars. The earliest period, the Noachian Age, may have been warm and wet, with active volcanoes. The Noachian Age corresponds with Noachis Terra, in the south of Mars, where the ancient uplands have been battered by meteorites. Next is the Hesperian Age, which became steadily colder, with water freezing. This age is named for the southern hemisphere's Hesperia Planum, which is considered younger because it shows less cratering. The present era is the Amazonian Age, named for the flat, low Amazonis Planitia of the north. This is a dusty desert region with relatively few craters and is one of the youngest on Mars.

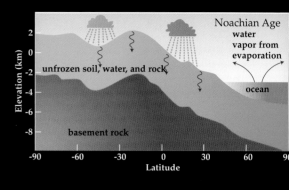

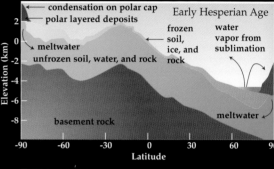

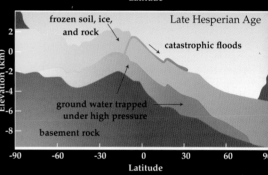

Noachian Mars

The Noachian era probably began about 4.5 billion years ago when Mars was formed and ended roughly 3.5 billion years ago. During this period meteorite cratering was slowing down. A warmer climate may have permitted rivers, lakes, and even oceans to exist on the surface.

MUCH AS IT WAS 3.5 BILLION YEARS AGO
A artist's panoramic view of Arabia Terra shows Schiaparelli Crater in the foreground. The area has changed little from Noachian times when meteorites were still raining down on the planet's surface.

WATER IN ABUNDANCE
Some scientists believe that the low plains of Mars's north polar regions might have been flooded by water flowing from the southern highlands in Noachian and Hesperian times. A thicker atmosphere could have held enough water vapor to produce rain.

WATER INTO ICE
In the Noachian Age (top), liquid water may have been present on the planet's surface and also underground. By the early Hesperian Age (middle), most water had seeped underground or was frozen on the surface. By the late Hesperian Age (bottom), much of the planet's water was locked up in underground ice deposits, but pockets of pressurized liquid water occasionally erupted on the surface to produce local breakouts or massive floods.

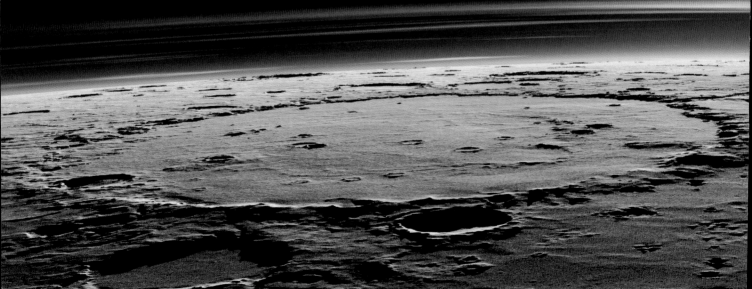

Hesperian Age

The Hesperian era lasted from about 3.5 billion years ago to 2.5 billion years ago. Volcanoes rumbled and lava flowed, but volcanic activity slowed down as Mars cooled. Water began freezing, forming ice on the surface and underground. In this time of change, there were probably torrential flash floods, which cut deep, wide channels. As water retreated underground and froze, Mars became drier, making a transition to another age.

AN AGE OF VOLCANOES

This illustration shows a Hesperian-era volcano in majestic eruption, sending smoke and ash into the sky. Such volcanic activity could have melted underground ice, causing floodwaters to suddenly burst out and scour deep channels in the Martian surface.

The Amazonian Age

The Amazonian era began about 2.5 billion years ago and extends to the present. During this period cratering and volcanic eruptions have continued but at lower levels than in previous ages. Today, Mars is dry and dusty, with a very thin atmosphere. One reason for this dryness is that atmospheric pressure is now so low that water reaching the surface freezes immediately or boils away. In this, the Amazonian Age, most of the water remaining on Mars is in the form of underground ice.

MARTIAN ROCK ON EARTH
This meteorite was discovered near Los Angeles in the 1970s. Scientific analysis found it originated on Mars. It is composed of lava and weighs just under a pound (452.6 g). It is only 175 million years old, proving that Martian volcanoes have been active in recent Amazonian times.

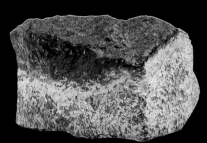

YOUTHFUL LOWLANDS
West of the Tharsis volcanic region is the low-lying Amazonis Planitia, which gives its name to the Amazonian Age. This photograph shows the lava-covered surface of the planitia, where fewer impact craters are found than in the older upland regions.

Martian atmosphere

THE "AIR," OR ATMOSPHERE, of Mars is much thinner than Earth's, and is 95 percent carbon dioxide. Earth's atmosphere is 78 percent nitrogen, 21 percent oxygen. The average Martian surface temperature is a bitterly cold minus 81°F (-63°C). In the upper Martian atmosphere, water and carbon dioxide vapors freeze and form high clouds. Other clouds appear over Mars when springtime winds puff dust into the air, causing great storms. Most of the grit settles down again, but fine reddish dust stays suspended in the atmosphere's lowest level—the "troposphere." Dust colors the sky a rose-orange. In the polar regions, suspended dust mingles with icy vapors and turns to snowy frost that covers the ground.

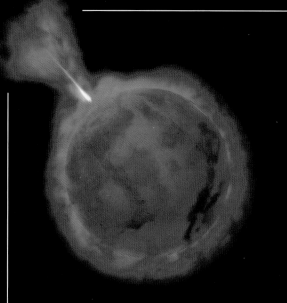

LOSING AIR IN NOACHIAN TIMES
Billions of years ago, meteor impacts blasted away much of the Martian atmosphere. Since then, air has continued to escape because the planet's gravity is just a third of Earth's. Weak gravity allows gases to vanish into space. Mars loses more atmosphere in winter, when carbon dioxide freezes to the polar caps, but in spring the carbon dioxide ice becomes a gas again.

SUNRISE THROUGH A HAZE
Martian air glows red in this artist's view of dawn as seen from orbit. Tiny particles bearing iron oxide float in the atmosphere, absorbing and scattering blue light but allowing red rays to get through. Mars's atmospheric pressure—the weight of its atmosphere—is only 1/143 of Earth's.

MARTIAN ATMOSPHERE

Composition

- Carbon dioxide about 95%
- Nitrogen about 2.7%
- Argon about 1.6%
- Oxygen, carbon monoxide, water vapor, and other gases about 0.7%

Structure

Thermosphere

81 miles/ 130 km

Stratosphere

Thin clouds of frozen carbon dioxide

Clouds of water ice particles

25 miles/ 40 km

Troposphere

Suspended red, iron-rich dust; fog of water ice particles

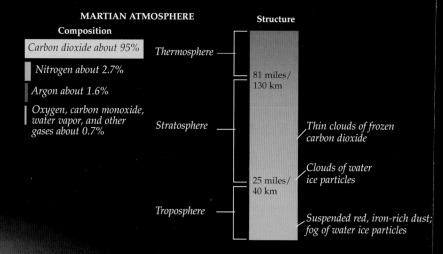

Clouds on Mars

Clouds form on the great volcanic peaks in summertime, when warmer air flows upward and cools. Water or carbon dioxide vapors form clouds over the polar caps and also at high altitudes. Clouds of water ice are found at 12–18 miles (19–29 km) high, and carbon dioxide clouds are at 30 miles (48 km). Because Mars is dry and cold, there is never rain, but in winter polar clouds leave frost on the ground and maybe snow.

MIST IN A LABYRINTH
Spacecraft cameras show early morning fog in Noctis Labyrinthus, canyons at the western end of Valles Marineris. The Martian atmosphere holds very little water vapor, but the combination of cold temperatures and low atmospheric pressure creates water ice clouds.

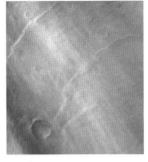

STREAKY CLOUDS
These clouds may appear anywhere on Mars, but are most common in the Syrtis Major highlands north of Hellas Planitia. Earth-based telescopes can see Martian clouds, which reflect sunlight and appear as bright spots.

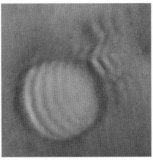

LEE WAVE CLOUDS
This photograph shows an example of a lee wave cloud over an impact crater. Lee wave clouds form around large obstacles such as mountains, ridges, craters, and volcanoes. The air in such regions often produces wavelike ripples.

Dust storms and "dust devils"

Martian winds are always at work scouring rocks and lifting dust. Clouds of dust can become powerful storms that cover thousands of miles. Dust clouds rise 3,000 feet (1 km) high and fill the air for weeks. Often, small whirlwinds—"convection currents"—spin into columns that twirl across the land. Termed "dust devils," they can be 300 feet (100 m) tall, and are visible to orbiting spacecraft.

MARTIAN TWISTER
Sunlight gleams off a spinning dust devil that is leaving a twisted trail behind it. Dust devils often form in summertime on the flat plains of Mars.

A DUST STORM GATHERS
The power of a smothering dust cloud is recorded in these 1999 images of a giant, swirling storm system over the north polar region. Taken two hours apart (from left to right), these pictures show the storm's rapid progress and turbulent expansion.

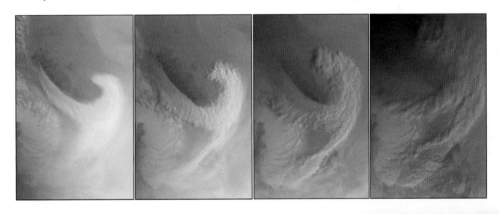

Does it snow on Mars?

In autumn, dense clouds blanket the northern polar region. This "polar hood" is difficult to see through, so scientists are not sure what is happening underneath. As winter sets in, the hood grows larger. Icy vapors freeze on the dust particles in the air, becoming snowlike crystals. When the polar hood shrinks, it leaves behind a white coating on the ground from frost and, possibly, snow.

SURPRISE SNOWFALL
An artist pictures a future astronaut studying surface ice on Mars when a light snow begins to fall. The astronaut reaches out to catch the flakes.

CONTRASTING SNOWFLAKES
A six-sided water-ice snowflake formed in Earth's atmosphere appears delicate and feathery beside this gemlike plastic model of a Martian carbon dioxide snowflake. Scientists know that frost regularly forms on Mars, but they are uncertain about whether or not snow occurs.

Snowflake on Earth

Martian snowflake

The moons of Mars

FOR CENTURIES, astronomers believed Mars had moons, but no one could find them. Anglo-Irish author Jonathan Swift accurately described Martian moons in his 1726 masterpiece, *Gulliver's Travels*, yet no one had ever seen them. In 1877, American astronomer Asaph Hall finally discovered the Martian moons. Hall found them with the powerful telescope of the United States Naval Observatory in Washington, D.C. He named them Phobos and Deimos after the sons of the Greek god Ares—the equal of the Roman Mars. These two tiny satellites are sometimes termed "moonlets." They may be asteroids, captured by Martian gravity. Hall called Phobos's largest crater "Stickney," his wife's maiden name.

AMAZING PREDICTION
British satirist and social critic Jonathan Swift (1667–1745) described the moons of Mars in 1726—more than 150 years before astronomers found them! His imaginary moons orbited at distances and speeds that turned out to be very similar to those of the actual moons.

Deimos

MOONLETS OF MARS
The two Martian satellites are shown here in artist's renderings. Phobos, the larger, is rough and cratered, with deep grooves, while Deimos appears a little smoother because its impact craters are partially buried by the rocks and dust blanketing its surface.

Stickney Crater

Phobos

IN ORBIT AROUND MARS
This painting imagines what Mars looks like from Phobos, the larger of the two Martian moons. The view is from 100 miles (160 km) above Phobos, which orbits at approximately 5,800 miles (9,400 km) above Mars.

Discoverer of the moons

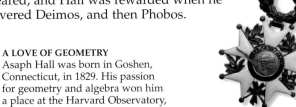

In August 1877, astronomer Asaph Hall studied the Red Planet night after night, searching for moons. Hall used the most powerful telescope of the time, but bad weather often blocked his view. When the weary Hall wanted to give up, his wife, Angeline Stickney Hall, urged him to keep trying. The weather finally cleared, and Hall was rewarded when he discovered Deimos, and then Phobos.

Arago Medal of the French Academie des Sciences

A LOVE OF GEOMETRY
Asaph Hall was born in Goshen, Connecticut, in 1829. His passion for geometry and algebra won him a place at the Harvard Observatory, Cambridge, Massachusetts, then at the U.S. Naval Observatory.

Legion of Honor

HONORS FOR DISCOVERY
Hall received several medals for his work, including France's Legion of Honor, the Arago Medal of the French Academie des Sciences, and the Gold Medal of the Royal Astronomical Society of Great Britain. In 1998, Hall's family donated his medals to the U.S. Naval Observatory in Washington, D.C.

Dimensions and orbits

Phobos is about 16 miles (27 km) on its long axis, while Deimos is 10 miles (16 km) long. Phobos orbits at more than 3,700 miles (6,100 km) above Mars. Deimos orbits at more than twice that distance away. Phobos orbits about three times a Martian day, while Deimos orbits once every 1.26 days. Scientists believe Phobos is slowly dropping and in 50 million years will crash onto Mars.

The satellites of Mars

This table shows the radius of each moon's orbit around Mars. It also shows the time each orbit takes, measured in Martian days, and the orbit speed. The moons' dimensions (length, width, and height) and surface area are also listed.

PROPERTY	DEIMOS	PHOBOS
Orbital radius	14,577 mi 23,459 km	5,827 mi 9,378 km
Orbital period	30 hrs 18 min	7 hrs 39 min
Mean orbital velocity	.87 mi/sec 1.4 km/sec	1.3 mi/sec 2.1 km/sec
Dimensions (miles) (kilometers)	10 x 7.5 x 6 16 x 12.5 x 10	16.1 x 13.7 x 11.5 26.8 x 22.8 x 19
Area	250 sq mi 400 sq km	625 sq mi 1,000 sq km

MOONSHADOW
The shadow of Phobos was captured by the Mars Orbiter Camera in 1999. The shadow is caused by Phobos's passing between Mars and the Sun, which often happens because the moon orbits Mars about every eight hours. This image covers an area 155 miles (250 km) across.

Deimos

Theoretical orbit of man-made satellite

Mars

MARTIAN LUNAR SYSTEM
In this chart, the orbits of the outer moon, Deimos, and inner moon, Phobos, bracket a third orbit. This additional orbit marks the course of a man-made satellite that would orbit at the same speed as Mars revolves on its axis. Seen from Mars, this satellite would always seem to stay in the same place.

Phobos

ESCAPE VELOCITY
Future astronauts could jump off Deimos into space. By just leaping upwards, they would reach an "escape velocity"—the speed needed to "escape" a gravitational field—of 18.7 feet per second (5.7 m/sec). Larger Phobos with its stronger gravity requires a leap of 33.8 feet per second (10.3 m/sec).

Mars Pathfinder

NASA LAUNCHED MARS PATHFINDER from Kennedy Space Center in Florida in December 1996, and the lander parachuted to the Martian surface on July 4, 1997. Protected by air bags, it bounced several times before settling down safely on Ares Vallis. The air bags deflated, the lander's three "petals" opened, and instruments began studying the surroundings. Ares Vallis, just north of the equator, was possibly an ancient channel where water had flowed. Sojourner, a robotic "surface microrover," drove from rock to rock, analyzing their chemical and physical makeup. Before power ran out three months later, Pathfinder and its rover sent back 2.6 gigabits of information about soil, rocks, and atmosphere, including 16,000 images. The mission was a great success, especially because Pathfinder had been expected to last only one month.

SUNSET ON MARS
In this photograph, the evening sky darkens as the end approaches to Pathfinder's day 24 on Mars—or 24th sol, as scientists term Martian days. The sun sets near the Twin Peaks, less than a mile from the landing site in Ares Vallis on the Chryse Planitia.

Ramps for Sojourner

IMP camera

Satellite dish

Solar panels

Protective shield

Weather monitor

PREPARING A SOFT LANDING
Before the mission, Pathfinder scientists examine the air bags that will inflate a few hundred feet above the surface to protect the spacecraft as it lands. Each bag is 17 feet (5 m) in diameter and composed of four separate bags that have six smaller spheres inside them.

Deflated air bags

PATHFINDER DEPLOYED
With air bags deflated and its three "petals" fully opened, the Mars Pathfinder lander is ready for research. Once a ramp is lowered, the rover will roll down and begin to study soil and rocks. The IMP camera, or Imager for Mars Pathfinder, is atop the tall mast on the lander.

Petal, with solar array

Twin Peaks

Antenna mast

Rover ramp

Sojourner Rover

"Six wheels on soil!" cried scientists on Earth when Sojourner rolled down its deployment ramp and onto Mars. This was the first "robotic roving vehicle" ever to explore Mars. The name, "Sojourner," honored the 19th-century African-American woman, Sojourner Truth, who fought against slavery and for women's rights. NASA's six-wheeled robotic explorer weighed about 24 pounds (11 kg) and was equipped with lasers, temperature sensors, cameras, telecommunications equipment, and tools for analyzing rock and dirt. Moving almost two feet (.6 m) a minute, the rover studied minerals on the ground and dust in the air. NASA scientists collecting Sojourner's data gave names like "Shark," "Wedge," "Squid," "Yogi," and "Chimp" to rocks the mission photographed.

SOJOURNER AT WORK
The rover's suspension system gives great stability, with joints that adjust as the ground changes. The suspension and six-wheel design allow Sojourner to cross a boulder 8 inches (20 cm) high—three times larger than a four-wheeler could cross. Sojourner can tip as much as 45 degrees to one side as it climbs a rock without falling over.

Large solar panel for power

Rock analyzer

Antenna

ROVER'S-EYE VIEW OF ITS LANDER
Sojourner photographs the Pathfinder Lander on sol 33. The IMP camera on the lander's mast is looking back at the rover. Deflated air bags stand out from this low angle, as does the rock "Ender," bottom, with "Hassock" behind it. "Yogi" is on the other side of the lander.

RED PLANET ALL AROUND
This 360-degree panorama of Ares Vallis was composed from several pictures taken by Pathfinder's IMP camera over three sols—8, 9, and 10. Stained by rust-colored dust, the air bags lie deflated under the lander's petals. Soil disturbed by Sojourner's wheels show a track leading away from a deployed ramp. The rover is directing its X-ray spectrometer at a basaltic rock that scientists named "Yogi."

Sojourner Rover

"Yogi" the rock

Deflated air bag

Mapping Mars

In the 1960s and 1970s, the Mariner and Viking missions led to the first topographic maps of Mars, and in 1997 the success of Mars Pathfinder furthered spacecraft technology. Later that year, Mars Global Surveyor provided detailed information on topography, gravity, and magnetic fields. Global Surveyor is NASA's most successful mapping mission. Yet planetary mapmaking involves more than charting mountains and canyons. Some scientific instruments used in mapping also identify minerals and frozen liquids. NASA's Mars Odyssey orbiter arrived in 2001 to map the surface, study minerals, and also look for water—which instrument readings suggested was there. Next came the European Space Agency's Mars Express orbiter in 2003. While mapping the South Polar cap, Mars Express confirmed Odyssey's finds of both water ice and carbon dioxide ice under the surface.

Mars Global Surveyor

At a height of 240 miles (380 km) Global Surveyor orbited the poles every two hours, employing three main instruments. The Mars Orbiter Camera took high-resolution images of surface features as small as 3 feet (1 m). The Thermal Emission Spectrometer studied the composition of rock, soil, ice, atmospheric dust, and clouds. Most important, the Mars Orbiter Laser Altimeter measured the heights of surface features, which were used to produce the most accurate Martian topographic map of all.

READYING GLOBAL SURVEYOR
Workers at NASA's Jet Propulsion Laboratory prepare Global Surveyor for transfer to a launch pad at the Cape Canaveral Air Station. The spacecraft is already mated to its booster launch vehicle, at bottom. After the launch, this booster rocket will fire and propel the spacecraft on its journey to the Red Planet. These workers will soon place Global Surveyor in a protective canister for movement to the pad.

High-gain antenna

Main engine on propulsion module

Winglike solar a

Drag flap for flight control

Scientific instrument payload

GLOBAL SURVEYOR'S COMPONENTS
Surveyor looks like a flying box with wing-like projections extending from opposite sides. When fully loaded with propellant—fuel—the spacecraft weighed 2,342 lbs (1,060 kg). Most of Surveyor's mass lies in the equipment module containing the spacecraft's science payload—electronics and science instruments. The propulsion module houses Surveyor's rocket engines and propellant tanks.

MAP PROJECTION OF MARS
NASA teams produced this mosaic map of Mars from
Global Surveyor data. The map uses more than
200 million Laser Altimeter measurements
and almost a thousand wide-angle Mars
Orbiter Camera images. The Altimeter
measurements show detail that
is not visible in photographic
images because of the dusty
Martian atmosphere.

Mars Odyssey

Odyssey mapped and analyzed the
Martian surface. NASA specially
equipped Odyssey to look for water
ice. The orbiter's Gamma Ray
Spectrometer was designed to
detect hydrogen—and therefore
water, which contains hydrogen.
Odyssey advanced the mapping of
Mars while also finding subsurface
water ice at both the north and
south polar regions.

ODYSSEY ABOVE MARS
Mars Odyssey weighed 1,671 pounds
(758 kg), fueled, and carried science
instruments. This orbiter studied the
Martian surface and climate and looked
for water. Odyssey also relayed data
transmissions from surface rovers back
to Earth.

Solar array

Antenna

*Gamma Ray
Spectrometer*

ODYSSEY MAPPING MARS
This thermal infrared image was
acquired as Mars Odyssey orbited
at 13,600 miles (22,000 km) high.
The 1,120-mile (1,800 km) wide Argyre
basin can be seen. The image spans 3,900
miles (6,276 km), from limb to limb.

Martian highs and lows

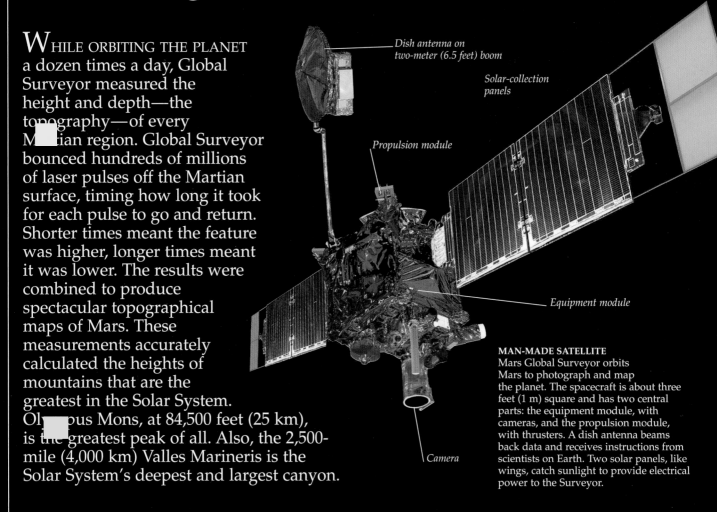

WHILE ORBITING THE PLANET a dozen times a day, Global Surveyor measured the height and depth—the topography—of every Martian region. Global Surveyor bounced hundreds of millions of laser pulses off the Martian surface, timing how long it took for each pulse to go and return. Shorter times meant the feature was higher, longer times meant it was lower. The results were combined to produce spectacular topographical maps of Mars. These measurements accurately calculated the heights of mountains that are the greatest in the Solar System. Olympus Mons, at 84,500 feet (25 km), is the greatest peak of all. Also, the 2,500-mile (4,000 km) Valles Marineris is the Solar System's deepest and largest canyon.

Dish antenna on two-meter (6.5 feet) boom

Solar-collection panels

Propulsion module

Equipment module

Camera

MAN-MADE SATELLITE
Mars Global Surveyor orbits Mars to photograph and map the planet. The spacecraft is about three feet (1 m) square and has two central parts: the equipment module, with cameras, and the propulsion module, with thrusters. A dish antenna beams back data and receives instructions from scientists on Earth. Two solar panels, like wings, catch sunlight to provide electrical power to the Surveyor.

OLYMPUS MONS
Almost 250 miles (402 km) below Global Surveyer lies Olympus Mons, which is more than three times higher than Mount Everest. At 374 miles (624 km) in diameter, Olympus Mons has 10 times the volume of Hawaii's Mauna Kea, the largest shield volcano on earth.

Global Surveyor's view of Mars

On these topographic maps, white indicates the highest terrain, the next lower is red, then yellow, green, and blue. Low northern plains, in blue, suggest young terrain, perhaps formed by lava flows. Few meteorite craters are visible in this region, but many are evident on older surfaces colored yellow. The western volcanic region shown in white and red towers over lower regions in yellow, green, and blue. One map presents a full hemisphere with the Tharsis Plateau and Valles Marineris. Two others show 0the North and South Poles. The rectangular map shows the entire surface of the planet.

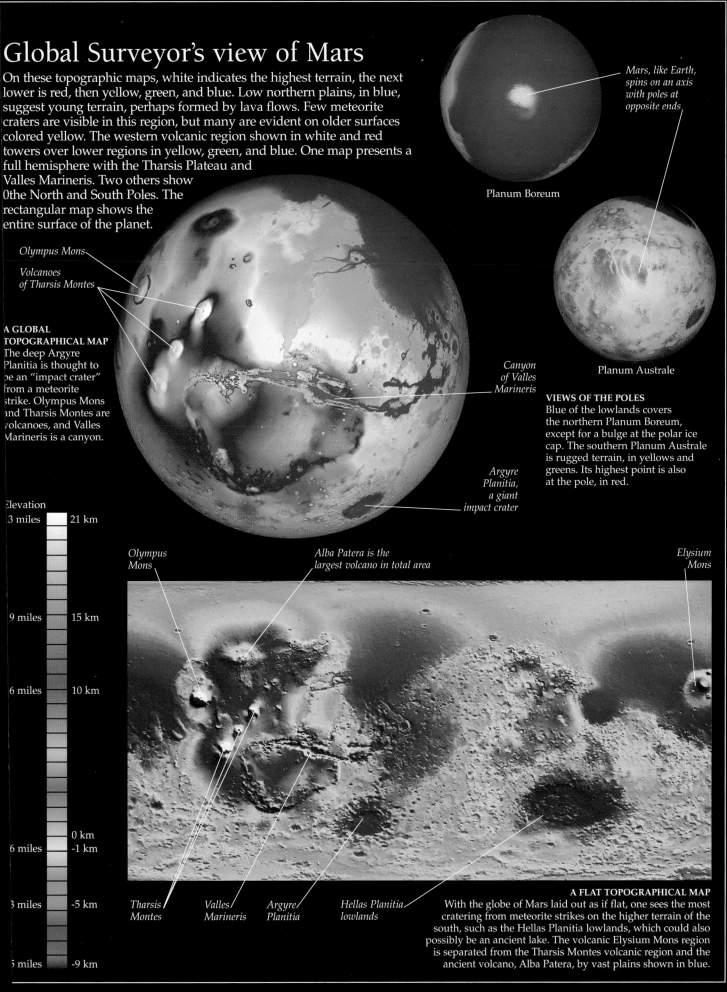

Olympus Mons

Volcanoes of Tharsis Montes

A GLOBAL TOPOGRAPHICAL MAP
The deep Argyre Planitia is thought to be an "impact crater" from a meteorite strike. Olympus Mons and Tharsis Montes are volcanoes, and Valles Marineris is a canyon.

Planum Boreum

Mars, like Earth, spins on an axis with poles at opposite ends

Planum Australe

Canyon of Valles Marineris

VIEWS OF THE POLES
Blue of the lowlands covers the northern Planum Boreum, except for a bulge at the polar ice cap. The southern Planum Australe is rugged terrain, in yellows and greens. Its highest point is also at the pole, in red.

Argyre Planitia, a giant impact crater

Elevation

3 miles	21 km
9 miles	15 km
6 miles	10 km
0 km	
6 miles	-1 km
3 miles	-5 km
5 miles	-9 km

Olympus Mons

Alba Patera is the largest volcano in total area

Elysium Mons

Tharsis Montes

Valles Marineris

Argyre Planitia

Hellas Planitia lowlands

A FLAT TOPOGRAPHICAL MAP
With the globe of Mars laid out as if flat, one sees the most cratering from meteorite strikes on the higher terrain of the south, such as the Hellas Planitia lowlands, which could also possibly be an ancient lake. The volcanic Elysium Mons region is separated from the Tharsis Montes volcanic region and the ancient volcano, Alba Patera, by vast plains shown in blue.

Polar ice caps

AFTER DISCOVERING the Martian polar ice caps in 1666, astronomers watched them grow larger in winter, smaller in summer. Observers were sure this was a freezing and melting process. They thought Mars must be like Earth, which has its own ice-covered poles. Astronomers in the 19th century mistakenly believed Martian canals were channeling polar water to cities in drier regions. In the late 20th century, space missions showed the polar caps to be encrusted with carbon dioxide ice. The poles can be as cold as 195°F (-126°C). Over millions of years, layer after layer of ice and dust have been deposited on the poles. By drilling through this ice, scientists may someday study the layers and learn about changes in the Martian climate.

North Polar Cap

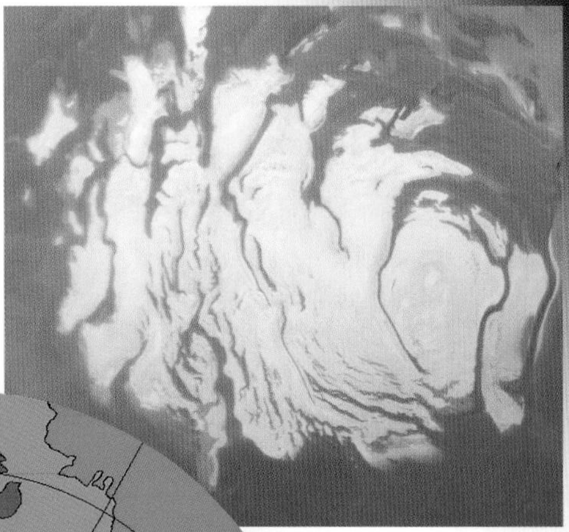

SOUTH POLAR CAP
Viking 2 made this image of the South Polar cap in 1977. Permanently frozen, the carbon dioxide ice cap stays about the same size all year. Global Surveyor data suggests a subcap of water ice underlies the cap. This water subcap is not exposed because during Mars's closest approach to the Sun the South Pole tilts away and is in darkness.

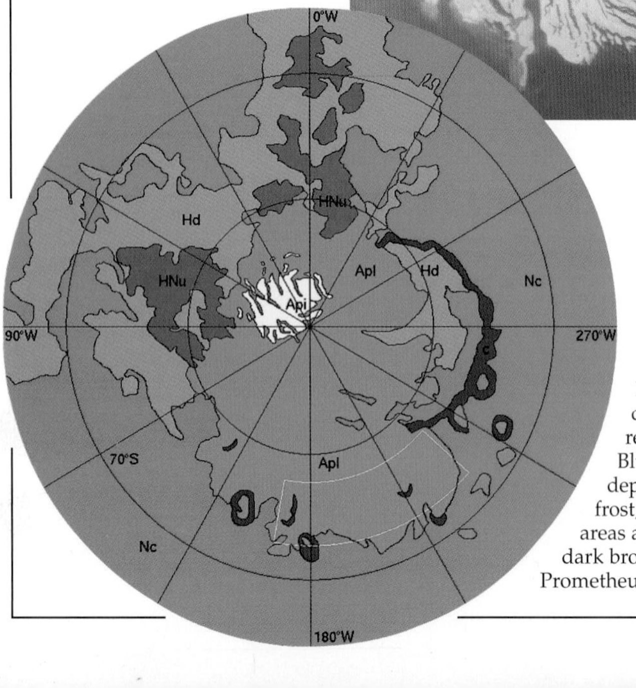

SOUTH POLE
The white area on this geologic map of the South Pole represents carbon dioxide ice deposits on the region called Planum Australe. Blue areas are layered ice deposits—mixtures of soil, dust, frost, and ice. Pink and purple areas are smooth plains, and the dark brown arc is the rim of the Prometheus impact basin.

NORTH POLE OF MARS
This artist's illustration shows the Planum Boreum region, with the North Polar cap in white. There are actually two caps, one permanent and one seasonal. The permanent cap, mainly water ice, is under a layer of carbon dioxide ice. This upper layer grows much larger in winter, then recedes as it melts each summer.

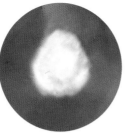

October 1996 January 1997 March 1997

DISAPPEARING ICE CAP

In winter, carbon dioxide in the Martian atmosphere freezes, much of it joining the North Polar cap, which grows larger. The first image—October 1996 on Earth—is early spring on Mars, with the cap at its greatest. Warming temperatures melt the cap, shown smaller in the late-spring middle image, and smallest in summertime. The great ring of dark sand dunes encircling the North Polar cap is now fully exposed.

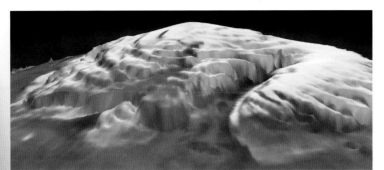

CLIFFS OF SOLID ICE

This three-dimensional representation of the North Polar cap appears like a great island of icy cliffs. The image was constructed by combining Viking orbiter photographs with topographic data from Mars Global Surveyor's Laser Altimeter.

Layers of ice, patterns of snow

The surface of the North Polar cap resembles a sponge, while the South Polar cap has large troughs and broad mesas. This indicates the poles have very different climates. The northern cap is warmer because it tilts sunward when Mars's elliptical orbit takes the planet closest to the Sun. In summer, the colder southern cap melts less than does the northern cap.

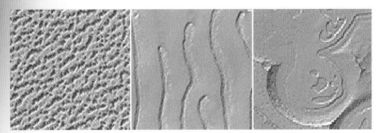

DESIGNS IN SNOW ON MARS

Martian snow patterns take on bizarre forms, and scientists often nickname them. The left image, from the North Polar region, is "Kitchen Sponge" because of its closely spaced pits, which are about 5.5 feet (1.7 m) deep. The wiggly designs, termed "fingerprints," are curved troughs on the South Polar cap. The next pattern, also from the south, is "Swiss Cheese."

ICE STACKED IN LAYERS

Mars has ice-bound soil and dust as deep as 10,000 feet (3.1 km). Some layers on this outcrop at the North Polar cap are 30–100 feet (9–30 m) thick. A single layer 33 feet (10 m) thick would take 100,000 years to accumulate.

FUTURISTIC EXPLORATION

This painting by a space scientist shows future astronauts using equipment to drill into polar ice. These researchers take core samples to study the different layers. In this same way, tree rings, ice cores, and sea-bottom cores are analyzed on Earth. Core samples help scientists learn about changes in a planet's climate over great time periods.

Canyons on Mars

THE SOLAR SYSTEM'S LONGEST CANYON NETWORK slashes 2,500 miles (4,023 km) from east to west across the surface of Mars. This great system of cracks and rifts is Valles Marineris—400 miles (644 km) at its widest, and four miles (7 km) down at its deepest. These canyons were formed by volcanic stresses on the Tharsis plateau region, where hot lava flowed, cooled, and then cracked. "Marsquakes" also opened the crust of the planet and deepened rifts and valleys. Water might once have flowed through Martian canyons, which now are swept by wind and dust. At the western end of Valles Marineris is Noctis Labyrinthus, a complex pattern of smaller fractures leading in every direction, like a maze— another name for a labyrinth.

(A) Volcanic era

(B) Permafrost exposed

(C) Evaporation and collapse

(D) Canyons and chasms

A SHUDDER AND ROAR
Mars rumbles with the power of an avalanche as canyon walls crumble into landslides. This illustration shows a towering cloud of dust rising as the wall of a Valles Marineris canyon suddenly gives way and collapses. Canyon floors are littered with avalanche debris.

FIRE, ICE, AND LANDSLIDES
These paintings show how, many millions of years ago, volcanic action built up the surface of the Tharsis region (A) and formed a bulge. Stress caused fractures—canyons—that broke the surface. These Marsquakes exposed layers of underground ice (B) that held the rock and soil together. Over time, the ice melted or evaporated (C), leaving the canyon walls unstable. Great landslides (D) tore down the walls, creating wider chasms—or "chasmas." This cycle of fracturing, evaporation, and landslides—and possible water flow—shaped Valles Marineris and other Martian canyon systems.

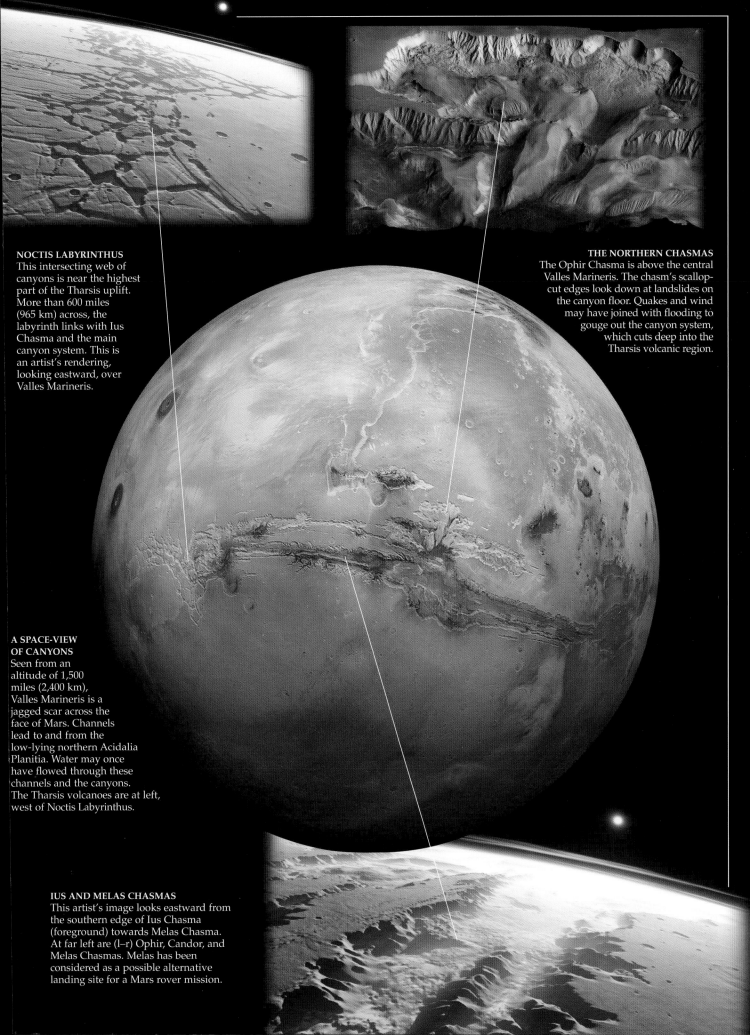

NOCTIS LABYRINTHUS
This intersecting web of canyons is near the highest part of the Tharsis uplift. More than 600 miles (965 km) across, the labyrinth links with Ius Chasma and the main canyon system. This is an artist's rendering, looking eastward, over Valles Marineris.

THE NORTHERN CHASMAS
The Ophir Chasma is above the central Valles Marineris. The chasm's scallop-cut edges look down at landslides on the canyon floor. Quakes and wind may have joined with flooding to gouge out the canyon system, which cuts deep into the Tharsis volcanic region.

A SPACE-VIEW OF CANYONS
Seen from an altitude of 1,500 miles (2,400 km), Valles Marineris is a jagged scar across the face of Mars. Channels lead to and from the low-lying northern Acidalia Planitia. Water may once have flowed through these channels and the canyons. The Tharsis volcanoes are at left, west of Noctis Labyrinthus.

IUS AND MELAS CHASMAS
This artist's image looks eastward from the southern edge of Ius Chasma (foreground) towards Melas Chasma. At far left are (l–r) Ophir, Candor, and Melas Chasmas. Melas has been considered as a possible alternative landing site for a Mars rover mission.

Craters on Mars

OVER BILLIONS OF YEARS, comets, asteroids, and meteorites have crashed by the thousands onto the Martian surface. From space, the planet looks pocked and scarred. Unlike Earth, Mars does not have the thick, protective atmosphere that burns up most space rocks. They blaze down and blast the Martian surface, creating "impact craters" that range from a few yards to hundreds of miles across. Impact craters have a circular ridge formed partly by debris thrown out in the explosion. As ages pass, craters are worn down by the work of weather. They are scoured by wind, filled with dust, and perhaps eroded by water. Some impact craters, such as Hellas Planitia, the planet's largest, could have become lakes filled with water. Even if a crater is eroded off the surface, the scar of the impact remains below ground.

BIRTH OF A CRATER
This illustration by a space scientist shows the power of an asteroid hitting Mars at 6 miles (10 km) a second. The massive explosion ejects debris into the air, blanketing the surroundings with rock and soil. This "ejecta" sometimes crashes down to make secondary impact craters.

CRATER FORMATION
It is not just the mechanical force of the impact that hurls debris in all directions when an asteroid or meteorite strikes. The space rock hits Mars faster than the speed of sound, so the impact creates enormous explosive energy, a fireball. This energy bursts out as a shock wave of heat, pressure, and mechanical force. This ejects, or throws out, debris that forms a blanketing layer around the crater. This layer is termed an "ejecta blanket."

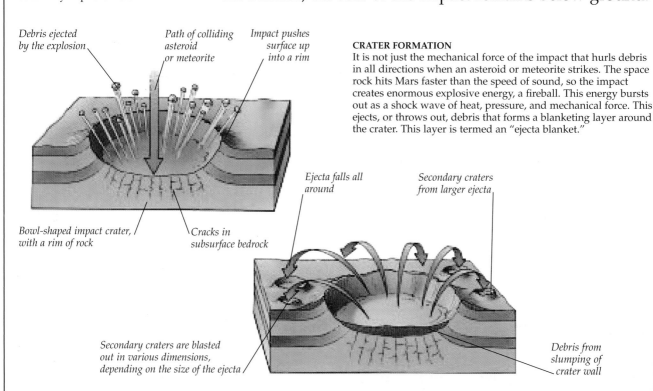

Debris ejected by the explosion

Path of colliding asteroid or meteorite

Impact pushes surface up into a rim

Bowl-shaped impact crater, with a rim of rock

Cracks in subsurface bedrock

Ejecta falls all around

Secondary craters from larger ejecta

Secondary craters are blasted out in various dimensions, depending on the size of the ejecta

Debris from slumping of crater wall

Floor of crater slowly rebounds, forming rings of ridges

Ejecta can fall in rays leading from crater

"Ejecta blanket" covers area around the crater

TIME-WORN CRATER
The rim of this impact crater is worn jagged by wind and weather. Surrounded by smaller, secondary-impact craters, it has rays formed from debris that was ejected by the explosion at first impact. Part of the crater floor has "bounced back" as circular high ground.

Variety of craters

Craters are classified by age, how they formed, or how they were affected by weather. "Rampart craters" have circular rims pushed up by an explosive impact and also lower, more irregularly shaped ramparts, or ridges, in the ejecta blanket surrounding the rim. An "exhumed" crater is a crater that has been partially or completely buried by dust or lava but later uncovered by wind or water action.

SECONDARY CRATERS
This crater cluster in Arabia Terra is over an area about 2 miles (3 km) wide. They could have been formed by the secondary impact of ejecta debris or by the breakup of a meteor as it disintegrated before striking Mars.

EXHUMED CRATER
Once buried under rock, soil, and dust, this "exhumed," or uncovered, crater was exposed by erosion. It has a thick mantle of dust, with dark streaks that show where dust has slumped down the crater walls. This crater, too, is in Arabia Terra.

SMILEY FACE
Well-known to astronomers as "Happy Face," this crater was photographed by Mars Global Surveyor. Named Galle Crater, it is on Argyre Planitia, itself one of the largest Martian impact craters. The bluish tones are winter frost.

RAMPART CRATER
When a meteorite slammed into Amazonis Planitia to create this rampart crater, the heat of the impact melted the layer of water ice, rock, and soil beneath the surface. Mud and rocks splashed out beyond the crater's rim and froze into a layered ejecta blanket with ramparts, or low ridges.

A YOUNG CRATER
Termed a "fresh impact crater," this meteorite crater in Arabia Terra shows rays of ejecta that have not yet been worn away by wind or covered with sand. The dark dots are boulders from ejecta debris.

MID-CRATER MOUNTAIN
The center of Gale Crater has risen over time to become a mountain. It is found in Terra Cimeria, south of Elysium Planitia and near the equator. A space artist pictured Gale Crater in the low light of sunset.

Volcanoes of Mars

VOLCANOES ARE VENTS that release melted rock, or magma, from underground. Magma rising through the mantle creates hot areas on the crust. Magma that breaks through the crust becomes lava. After flowing out of a volcano, lava cools and hardens, sometimes spreading hundreds of miles. Martian volcanoes once spewed out huge quantities of hot gas and water vapor, thickening the atmosphere. Clouds of cooling water vapor may have turned to liquid water, creating seas, lakes, and rivers. Most Martian volcanoes have been inactive for 40–100 million years, but some may have erupted within the past 10 million years—or even within half a million years. Volcanoes are found in three regions: the Tharsis region, Elysium Planitia, and Hellas Planitia.

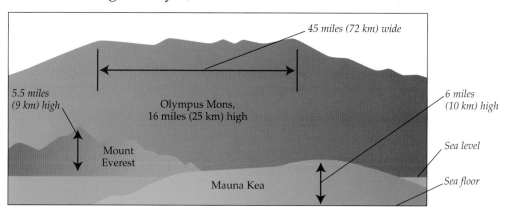

45 miles (72 km) wide

5.5 miles (9 km) high

Olympus Mons, 16 miles (25 km) high

6 miles (10 km) high

Mount Everest

Sea level

Sea floor

Mauna Kea

OLYMPUS MONS CALDERA
The caldera, or summit crater, of Olympus Mons averages about 50 miles (80 km) across, with walls as deep as 1.75 miles (2.8 km). Calderas are produced when the magma chamber collapses, usually during eruptions. This overhead image is from the Mars Express High Resolution Stereo Camera.

ABOVE EARTH'S GIANTS
Earth's highest mountain, Mount Everest in the Himalayas, and largest volcano, Mauna Kea in Hawaii, would be swallowed up in Olympus Mons. This long-extinct volcano, the largest in the solar system, stands three times higher than airliners fly above Earth.

SUNRISE OVER OLYMPUS
Majestic Olympus Mons, with a diameter of 400 miles (640 km), is the highest region on Mars. Rising to 16 miles (25 km), it is three times higher than any landform on Earth. This artist's perspective is from west to east, with a section of the volcano's great cliffs in shadow. Olympus Mons covers an area approximately equal to the state of Kansas.

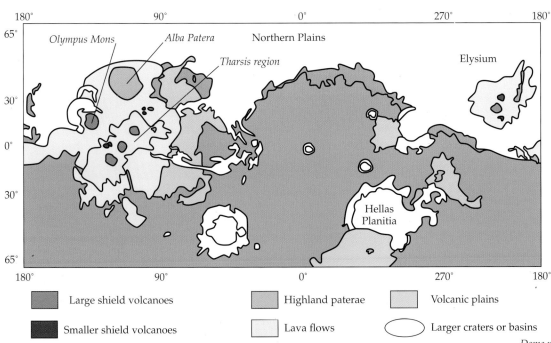

Large shield volcanoes	**Highland paterae**	**Volcanic plains**
Smaller shield volcanoes	**Lava flows**	**Larger craters or basins**

LANDS OF VOLCANISM
The main volcanic regions, Tharsis and Elysium, are in yellow. The third, much smaller region of pateras is near Hellas Planitia. Volcanoes termed "patera"—saucer-like, because they are flat—are much older than the volcanoes of Tharsis and Elysium. Alba Patera has the largest base—930 miles (1,500 km) across—but is less than 4.3 miles (7 km) high. The entire Tharsis region is 2,500 miles (4,000 km) across.

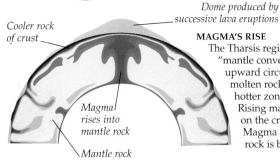

MAGMA'S RISE
The Tharsis region was created by "mantle convection." This is an upward circulation of underground molten rock, or magma, from a hotter zone beneath the mantle. Rising magma creates a hot spot on the crust where lava erupts. Magma here is red; cooler mantle rock is blue, green, and yellow.

Dome produced by successive lava eruptions

Cooler rock of crust

Magma rises into mantle rock

Mantle rock

FLOW OF FIRE AND WATER
In a painting of early Mars an artist pictures a lake at the foot of an erupting volcano. A great plume of ash rises from the cone as molten lava flows toward an inlet. Rock formations were formed by previous lava flows.

Various volcanoes

Some volcanoes erupt in explosions that throw out ash, gases, and rock that build steep slopes, termed "flanks." These slopes may be eroded by weather and cut by new rushes of lava. Other volcanoes steadily release lava that cools into gentle slopes shaped like a flattened dome or a shield. Most Martian volcanoes, like Olympus Mons, are the shield type.

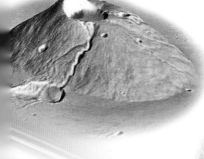

CERAUNIUS THOLUS
This steep volcanic cone was likely built up by explosive eruptions of porous volcanic ash, which is easily eroded. Later streams of upwelling molten lava cut channels in the cone's sides, and meteorites pocked it with impact craters. Ceraunius Tholus is in the northern Tharsis region, between Alba Patera and the three great shield volcanoes of Tharsis Montes.

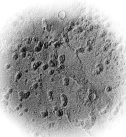

HELLAS MOUNDS
Mounds near Hellas Planitia may have been caused by superheated mud rising explosively to the surface.

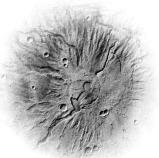

TYRRHENA PATERA
The shallow, eroded slopes of this patera volcano may be composed of ash deposits instead of repeated lava flows.

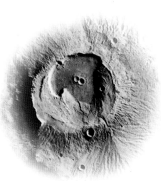

APOLLINARIUS PATERA
An initial ash eruption created the steep sides of this volcano. Later, molten lava formed a fan on the south flank.

Dunes on Mars

As FINE, WIND-BLOWN dust rises into the Martian atmosphere, the heavier particles settle to the surface to fill gullies and craters. Some particles pile up into dunes that are shaped and sculpted by the winds. Sand and dust are whipped into amazing, changing forms that are captured in photographs from orbiting spacecraft. Most Martian dunes are dark, composed of ground-up volcanic rock. Their patterns are especially fascinating in spring, when carbon dioxide frost on the dunes begins to melt. Seen from high above, the withdrawing ice creates fantastic designs that cover hundreds of miles of surface. Since Martian gravity is only a third of Earth's, dunes can grow twice as high as those on Earth. The largest dunes on Mars surround the northern polar ice field in a great ring 80 feet (24 m) high.

DUNE GULLIES
This Mars Global Surveyor image shows mysterious gullies that stripe sand dunes of Russell Crater in the southern highlands. How these gullies were formed is unknown. They occur mostly on south-facing slopes.

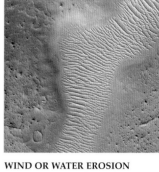

WIND OR WATER EROSION
In this photo, the floor of southern Auqakuh Vallis—an ancient valley—is covered by ripple-like forms made by the wind. This site, in Arabia Terra, might have been carved out by flowing water that has long since vanished.

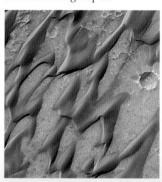

SCOURED AND TANGLED
Wind-scoured sand dunes in central Herschel Crater were imaged by the Mars Orbiter Camera of Mars Global Surveyor. These dunes appear to be cemented solidly into twisted, ribbonlike shapes.

FROST ON THE SAND
This springtime photo shows eroded dunes covered by carbon dioxide frost that is beginning to "sublime" away, or evaporate into the air. Retreating frost often leaves streaks on dunes, that look like works of abstract art.

Polar dunes

The northern polar regions are flat seas of sand swept by the wind, and dunes can take on complex and bizarre geometric patterns. Designs are especially spectacular in regions where prevailing winds change directions with the passing seasons. Dunes of the south polar regions are much smaller, and are usually found in craters and ravines.

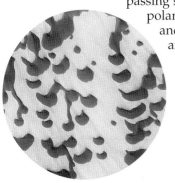

A NORTHERN CHASM
In this photo, summertime highlights crescent-shaped sand dunes in Chasma Boreale, a wide trough in the north polar region. Frost has retreated now, revealing dark-colored sand. The curved side of each dune is facing the direction in which the wind is blowing. This side is known as the slipface. Sand and dust pile up here until the wind changes direction and forms a different slipface.

FORTUNE-COOKIE DUNES
So named because many resemble Chinese fortune cookies, these north polar dunes have steep slipface slopes that are directed to the upper left. This area was photographed by the Mars Global Surveyor.

DIZZYING DUNES
The imaginary astronaut in this artist's rendering tramps through sand dunes that the wind has swirled into wavy ripples. The scene was inspired by actual dune formations in Death Valley, California, which compare to some types of sand dunes on Mars.

RUST-COLORED PANORAMA
This painting shows a Martian desert in all its ruddy glory, with the sky colored by fine, suspended dust. Only a swirling dust devil or two bring movement to this desolate scene of rocks, dunes, and wind-blown sand.

Rivers on Mars

Liquid WATER IS needed for life as we know it, but Mars is drier than any desert on Earth. Mars is too cold and its atmosphere is too thin for water to exist except as ice or vapor. Yet scientists believe the planet once had a milder climate, with rivers emptying into lakes and seas. Some Martian landforms could be from a watery era 3,500 million years ago. These landforms include ancient drainage networks that seem cut by flowing water. Also, Mars has deposits of soil and debris normally found at river mouths, and there are flat regions that could have been floors of now-vanished lakes or seas. Martian terrain is often similar to arid regions on Earth, such as Asian deserts that once had their own rushing rivers and streams.

RIVERS FLOW IN NOACHIAN MARS
Muddy floods in ancient Mars would have looked like this artist's rendering of water-filled river channels at Chryse Planitia. Water from melting snow and ice is shown flowing through Kasei Vallis in the background. Layers of sediment would have been deposited and later exposed when the water evaporated or flowed away.

WATER'S HIGHWAY
Curving landforms may have been shaped by the surging might of a Martian flood. This artist's rendering is of a dry riverbed in a mountain valley once swept with rushing water released from a reservoir of melting ice, perhaps heated by an erupting volcano. Surrounding the valley floor are rock formations that have been scoured by wind and dust.

ANCIENT LAKE AND VALLEY
Gusev Crater, at left, may be a former lake fed by the snaking Ma'adim Vallis. The crater is about 100 miles (160 km) across and is the landing site for the Spirit Rover. Impact features within the crater have been filled and smoothed over, probably with sediment deposited by water from the 560-mile (900 km) Ma'adim canyon.

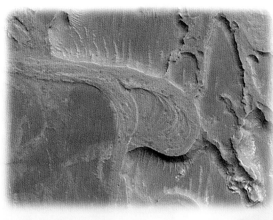

MEANDERING SEDIMENT
Comparisons with sediment formations on Earth suggest that this rockform southeast of Valles Marineris was originally sand deposited in a liquid environment. The sediment's loop shape appears to have been formed by a meandering—winding—stream. Sediment hardens over millions of years and turns to "sedimentary" rock. This particular rockform is termed a "meander" and is convincing evidence that water once flowed here.

Lost rivers of ancient days

Scientists search for evidence of water on Mars by comparing Earth's dried-up waterways with Martian features. Southwest Asia's long-empty river beds look much like dendritic—branching—channels found on Mars. Other landforms indicating past water on Mars are deposits of sediment seemingly left by enormous floods.

South Yemeni dendritic system

EMPTY STREAMS ON EARTH AND MARS
Scientists believe the above image shows an ancient river drainage system on Mars. The branchlike network in the image at right is a former river in South Yemen, one of the driest places on Earth. Martian dendritic channels could have been cut by water flowing under a protective cover of ice.

Water on Mars

SCIENTISTS BELIEVE WATER once flowed on Mars, forming rivers and lakes, even causing floods. As the planet cooled billions of years ago, the water evaporated, froze, or sank beneath the surface. Instruments on orbiting spacecraft, such as Odyssey and Mars Express, have detected hydrogen in the Martian soil. This suggests water ice is near the surface. Hydrogen-rich soil is especially common in volcanic regions, in the canyons of Valles Marineris, and at the poles. Some northern polar soils are estimated to be 50 percent water. This means a pound of soil would yield half a pound of water if heated. Farther underground, where temperatures are warmer, liquid water might exist. Also, subsurface mineral salts could dissolve in underground water and keep it from freezing.

A WATERY PLANET IN NOACHIAN TIMES
This painting shows how Mars might have appeared 3.5 billion years ago, partially covered with water. At bottom left is submerged Hellas Planitia. The northerly Utopia Planitia, and Isidis Planitia at left, are part of a great sea. Near its shores stand the Elysium volcanoes; top to bottom: Hecates Tholus, Elysium Mons, and Albur Tholus.

TEARDROP MESA
Landforms on Mars take strange and interesting shapes. This image from the European Space Agency's Mars Express orbiter shows a teardrop-shaped mesa—a high, flat-topped formation. Found in Chryse Planitia, it likely was an island, with water flowing past. The double impact craters were caused by later meteorite strikes.

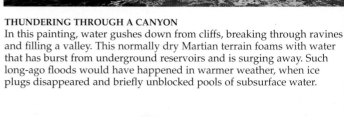

Impact craters

FORMING CLIFF GULLIES
Under the Martian surface, near a crater or canyon wall, water might be present along with ice, rock, and soil in a "semi-permeable" layer. If a barrier plug of ice melted and turned to vapor, the water would rush downhill, creating gullies.

THUNDERING THROUGH A CANYON
In this painting, water gushes down from cliffs, breaking through ravines and filling a valley. This normally dry Martian terrain foams with water that has burst from underground reservoirs and is surging away. Such long-ago floods would have happened in warmer weather, when ice plugs disappeared and briefly unblocked pools of subsurface water.

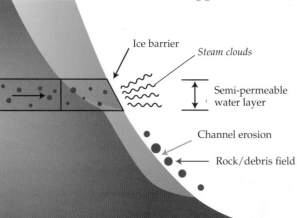

Ice barrier

Steam clouds

Semi-permeable water layer

Channel erosion

Rock/debris field

HIGHLAND GULLIES
Many gully systems are found high on Martian ridges. Some systems seem recent, with sharply cut features that cross older, wind-scoured erosion. These recent systems could have been made by meltwater running under a protective covering of snow or by water that burst from underground channels in periods of warmer weather.

46

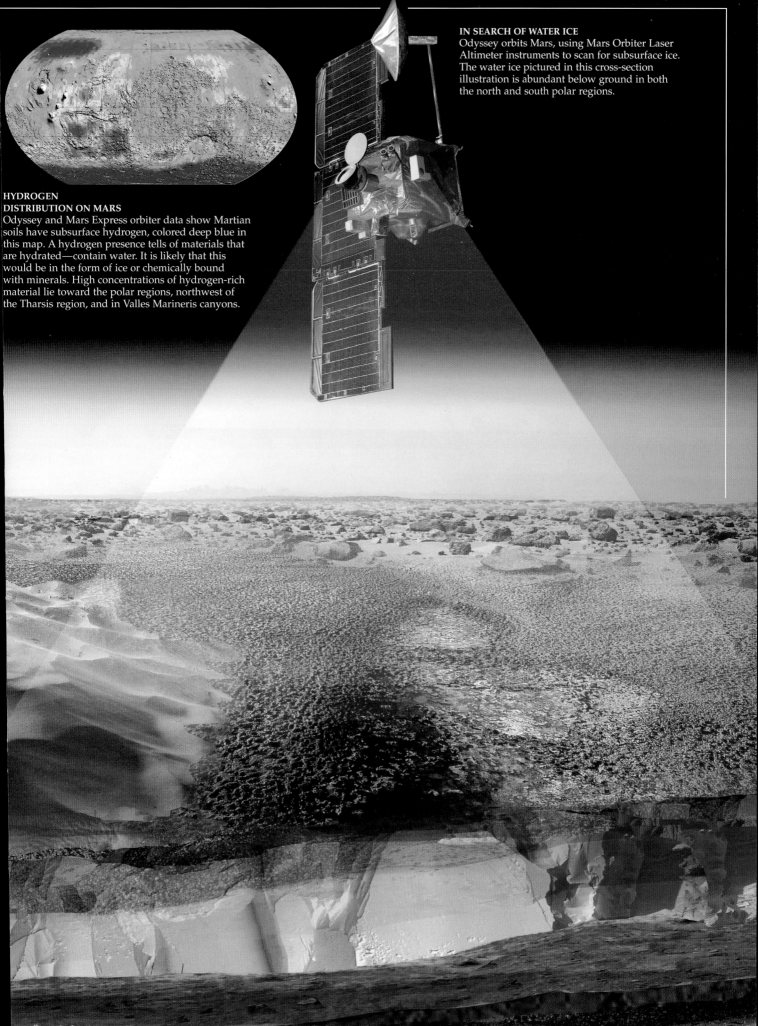

IN SEARCH OF WATER ICE
Odyssey orbits Mars, using Mars Orbiter Laser Altimeter instruments to scan for subsurface ice. The water ice pictured in this cross-section illustration is abundant below ground in both the north and south polar regions.

HYDROGEN DISTRIBUTION ON MARS
Odyssey and Mars Express orbiter data show Martian soils have subsurface hydrogen, colored deep blue in this map. A hydrogen presence tells of materials that are hydrated—contain water. It is likely that this would be in the form of ice or chemically bound with minerals. High concentrations of hydrogen-rich material lie toward the polar regions, northwest of the Tharsis region, and in Valles Marineris canyons.

Meteorites from Mars

SCIENTISTS HAVE FOUND and closely studied a number of rocks believed to have come to Earth from Mars. Hundreds of millions of years ago, asteroids or comets crashed down on Mars and sent shattered rock flying. The planet's weak gravity allowed some pieces of rock to escape and drift through space. After many millions of years, a few were captured by Earth's gravity and pulled downward. They sped through the thick atmosphere as meteors, and many burned up from heat caused by friction. Others survived to hit Earth's surface. These are termed "meteorites"—space rocks that have reached Earth. Meteorites from Mars are found mainly in Antarctica and Africa. At least one Martian meteorite shows signs of having been in liquid water long ago, and some scientists suspect that it may contain tiny fossilized life-forms.

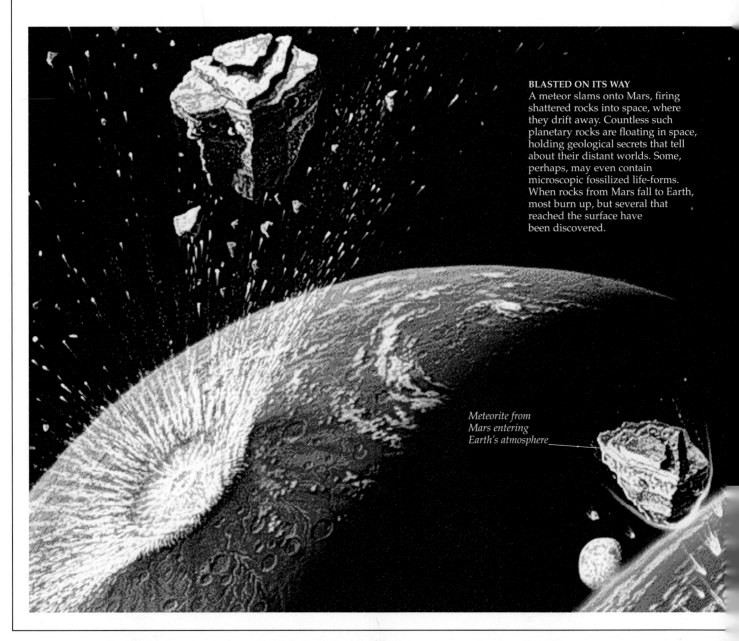

MARS TO CALIFORNIA
This meteorite was one of two found near Los Angeles in the 1970s. Weighing just over half a pound (245 g), it was first identified in 1999 as having come from Mars. By then, meteors from 14 places on Earth had been identified as Martian, including one originally found in France in 1815.

BLASTED ON ITS WAY
A meteor slams onto Mars, firing shattered rocks into space, where they drift away. Countless such planetary rocks are floating in space, holding geological secrets that tell about their distant worlds. Some, perhaps, may even contain microscopic fossilized life-forms. When rocks from Mars fall to Earth, most burn up, but several that reached the surface have been discovered.

Meteorite from Mars entering Earth's atmosphere

Martian meteorites have been discovered on most continents, especially in Africa. Most meteorites weigh less than a pound (450 g). This 55-pound (25 kg) stone (right) from Libya's Sahara Desert is part of the largest known Martian meteorite, which weighs about 210 pounds (95 kg). Named Dar al Gani, this meteorite shattered into hundreds of fragments upon impact. The photograph at left shows the Sahara Desert, where the meteorite was found.

Finding Martian rocks in Antarctica

One of the best places on Earth to look for meteorites is the frozen southern continent of Antarctica. To prove Martian origins, geochemists look for microscopic air bubbles in meteorites with the same exact mixture of gases as the Red Planet's atmosphere.

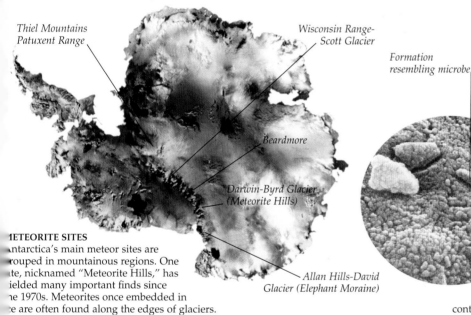

Thiel Mountains Patuxent Range

Wisconsin Range- Scott Glacier

Formation resembling microbe

Beardmore

Darwin-Byrd Glacier (Meteorite Hills)

Allan Hills-David Glacier (Elephant Moraine)

METEORITE SITES
Antarctica's main meteor sites are grouped in mountainous regions. One site, nicknamed "Meteorite Hills," has yielded many important finds since the 1970s. Meteorites once embedded in ice are often found along the edges of glaciers.

OLDEST METEORITE
Found in the Allan Hills during the 1984–1985 Antarctic summer, this meteorite is cataloged as ALH 84001. In 1994, researchers found it to be 4.5 billion years old, the most ancient Martian meteorite yet known.

EVIDENCE OF LIFE?
This electron microscope image of a carbonate formation in ALH 84001 shows wormlike shapes that some scientists believe could be fossilized microbes—microscopic life-forms. Other scientists disagree, saying they are inorganic mineral formations. Heated debates continue to rage over these unexplained structures.

CARBONATES IN ALH 84001
A microscopic cross-section of ALH 84001 shows carbonate formations, which contain the controversial wormlike structures. Carbonate structures form in water, suggesting that ALH 84001 was almost certainly exposed to water for a long time.

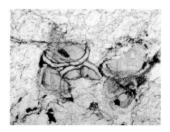

Meteorite on ice surface

A FIND ON ANTARCTICA
Every year, in the summer months, international meteorite hunters stage expeditions to Antarctica. This 2001 field team from the Antarctic Search for Meteorites (ANSMET) organization examines a newly discovered space rock. ANSMET is sponsored by the U.S. National Academy of Sciences, NASA, and the Smithsonian Institution.

Is there life on Mars?

QUESTIONS ABOUT MARTIAN LIFE began when early astronomers thought the planet was much like Earth. Later observers imagined they saw canals and vegetation in their telescopes. A few said Martians might be more advanced than humans. Then orbiters and robotic rovers found Mars to be a frozen desert with no living organisms. Scientists began to look for signs of past life, especially where water once flowed. Their instruments discovered ice, and their studies delved into Martian rocks on the planet and Martian meteorites on Earth. Since microscopic life-forms exist in Earth's most extreme regions, then microorganisms might also exist on Mars. The planet has "hot spots" that might be geothermal vents. These, some scientists say, may be among the best places to look for Martian life.

SPOTS ON POLAR ICE
These blotches on polar ice in springtime are thought to be caused by frost withdrawing. A few scientists, however, think certain of these patterns could be caused by living microorganisms that change their forms with warmer weather. Bacteria living in Antarctic ice create similar patterns. On Mars some patterns change even in places where frost does not withdraw.

SNOW ALGAE ON EARTH
Tiny plantlike organisms called algae thrive in places on Earth where no other living things can exist. Some are in hot springs, where water boils. Others, like this snow algae, *Chlamydomonas nivalis,* survive in bitterly cold conditions comparable to the Martian environment. Researchers believe such primitive organisms might be found on Mars.

REULL VALLIS GULLIES
The winding channel of Reull Vallis, imaged by Mars Express orbiter in 2004, empties into the Hellas basin. If water ever flowed through this canyon, then living creatures may also have been here. Fossil microorganisms might be present in the soil at the bottom of the canyon, in cracked rocks there, or in ice deposits beneath the surface.

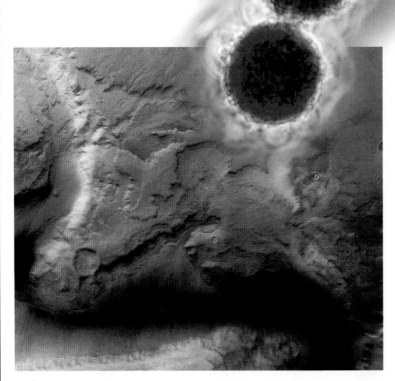

Ice towers on Mars

Some researchers insist the key place to look for life on Mars is where "geothermal hot spots" seem to be. These are places with higher ground temperatures than their surroundings. They might be volcanic vents releasing subsurface warmth. In Earth's Antarctic regions, such vents create chimneys of ice that tower above the snowfields. Inside them microscopic organisms may find shelter from severe polar weather.

Hellas Planitia (basin)

Thermal anomalies

THERMAL ANOMALIES

Mars Odyssey orbiter's heat-sensing camera has recorded what seem to be areas warmer than their surroundings—"thermal anomalies." These unexplained warm places are found in the Hellas basin. They are 10°F (5.5°C) warmer than the materials around them, and they stay warmer both night and day. They could be similar to volcanic vents in Antarctica.

TOWERS OF ICE—AND LIFE?

If the Hellas basin has geothermal heat vents, they might look like the ice towers in this painting. Martian towers could soar to 100 feet (30 m) because of the planet's weak gravity. Icy walls would filter out harmful radiation, and volcanic gases could provide needed heat and chemical energy for primitive life forms to endure for millions of years.

ICY CHIMNEYS

Hollow towers of ice form on the steaming volcanic vents of Mount Erebus, a volcano on Ross Island, Antarctica. Towers built up by the freezing of steam from the vents rise as high as 33 feet (10 m). Volcanic heat keeps inside temperatures at around freezing, so microorganisms could thrive there, sheltered from fierce winds and cold.

Mars rovers and Martian rocks

NASA LAUNCHED two Mars Exploration Rover spacecraft in mid-2003, each carrying identical rovers. The prime mission of these two "robotic field geologists," as Spirit and Opportunity rovers were described, was to find signs of past water activity. Spirit arrived in Gusev Crater on January 4, 2004. Opportunity landed halfway around the Martian globe on Meridiani Planum on January 25. Equipment on their Instrument Deployment Devices—robotic arms—drilled rock and took the first-ever microscopic photographs on Mars. Each rover drove thousands of yards around its landing site. The search for evidence of water was a resounding success, particularly with the discovery of minerals that usually form in groundwater. Opportunity found sedimentary rock that had been laid down in liquid, probably water. Scientists are gaining confidence that Mars could have once supported life.

ROBOTIC GEOLOGISTS
Spirit and Opportunity are six-wheel-drive rovers with a speed of 120 inches (300 cm) a minute. They are 5.2 feet (1.6 m) long, weigh 384 pounds (174 kg), and are ideal mobile geological laboratories. The rovers carry panoramic stereo cameras, spectrometers, and a magnetic dust collector. Telecommunications and computer equipment let them operate independently of their landers.

PANORAMA OF EAGLE CRATER
Opportunity Rover's stony Martian laboratory is seen in this 360-degree panorama of Eagle Crater, the landing site at Meridiani Planum. Many of the rock outcroppings on the crater's floor and walls were studied and given descriptive names such as "El Capitan" and "Berry Bowl." Opportunity eventually had to find its way out of the crater by carefully climbing over the rim.

LANDING SITE A DRY SEABED
Opportunity landed on Meridiani Planum, one of the smoothest, flattest regions on Mars. This high plain may once have been a shallow, salty sea, as depicted in this painting.

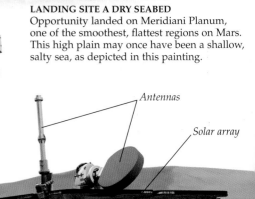

Cameras and spectrometer on mast

Instrument Deployment Device

Antennas

Solar array

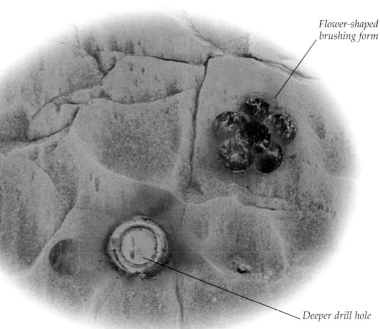

Flower-shaped brushing form

Deeper drill hole

A ROCK NAMED "MAZATZAL"
On its 76th day on Mars—sol 76—Spirit approached Mazatzal, the light-toned boulder 6.6 feet (200 cm) wide that spans this image. After closely studying data collected by Spirit's instruments, scientists on Earth found indications of past water in this rock. Mazatzal was named for a mountain range in Arizona.

CLOSE UP VIEW OF MAZATZAL
Spirit's Rock Abrasion Tool (RAT) brushed surface dust from six points on Mazatzal's surface. The brushing created a flower shape that gave room for spectrometer examination. Deeper RAT drilling exposed interior rock for microscopic photographs that showed tiny cracks containing evidence of water's presence long ago.

Blueberry-like rock formations

"BERRY BOWL" STONE SHAPES
On sol 42, Opportunity moved along a rock outcrop leading from El Capitan and arrived at a formation named "Berry Bowl." About the size and shape of BB pellets, blueberry-like formations there appear to have been deposited in salty water. The mineral hematite, which usually forms in the presence of water, was found here. NASA put this image in "false color" to make the stones look like berries. This is achieved through the use of infrared, green, and violet filters.

LAYERS CREATED UNDER WATER
On its 41st sol, Opportunity used the Microscopic Imager to show details of this rock in Eagle Crater. The layers display "crossbedding" features that occur on Earth when sediment is laid down by flowing water. In this crater, the rover found jarosite, a mineral that needs water to take form.

Unsuccessful missions

In 1960, THE SOVIETS launched Marsnick 1, mankind's first probe to Mars. That probe failed, as did the next eight Soviet spacecraft. Their tenth launch achieved orbit, but its lander crashed. The Soviet program ended in 1988 after three successes and 15 flops. The United States, on the other hand, launched 16 Mars missions before 2004, with 11 successes. Almost two-thirds of the first 37 Mars missions—including one each by Russia, Japan, and the ESA—failed completely or in part. Some fizzled at launch, while others reached Mars but did not complete their missions. The reasons for many losses are unknown, as is the case with Mars Express, launched by the European Space Agency. Express achieved orbit in 2004, but lost contact with its lander, Beagle 2.

PHOBOS 1
The Soviets launched Phobos 1 and 2 in 1988 to examine the moon Phobos. After a computer error misdirected its solar array away from the Sun, Phobos 1 lost all power. Phobos 2 was supposed to come within 150 feet (50 m) of the moon and send down two landers. In the final stage of its mission, communication was lost because of a computer breakdown.

THE PLAN FOR BEAGLE 2
If it had succeeded, Beagle 2, the Mars Express lander, would have looked like this artist's rendering. The lander is shown safely deployed on Isidis Planitia, at the planned landing site it probably never reached. On December 25, 2003, Mars Express entered orbit, and Beagle 2 began its descent, but contact was lost and never regained.

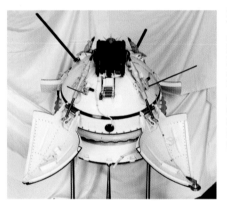

MARS 2 LANDER
The Soviets' Mars 2 descent/lander module was launched in 1971 to study the Martian surface and clouds and measure the magnetic field. When the lander was released on November 27, the descent system did not work properly, and it crashed. Mars 2 became the first man-made object on the surface of Mars.

MARS 3 SPACECRAFT
The landers of the Soviets' Mars 2 and Mars 3 failed in late 1971, but both spacecraft went into orbit. For several months, they sent valuable data back to Soviet space centers. The Mars 3 orbiter and descent module, shown here, are 13.5 feet (4.1 m) tall and weigh about 10,250 pounds (4,650 kg) when filled with fuel. The descent module is at the top, the propulsion system at the bottom. The wings are solar arrays.

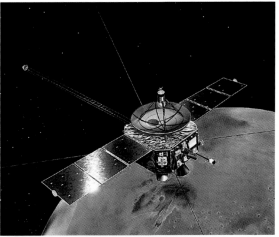

NOZOMI
Another series of mission failures began in 1998, starting with Japan's Nozomi orbiter, which was equipped to study the Martian upper atmosphere. The orbiter is 1.9 feet (.58 m) high, with a dish antenna and solar panel wings. Japanese for "Hope," Nozomi needed unplanned maneuvers that consumed too much fuel. The craft did not make it into a Mars orbit and instead is orbiting the Sun.

MARS CLIMATE ORBITER
Another disappointment, this orbiter was launched by NASA in 1998 to work with the Mars Polar Lander (see below), studying weather and atmosphere. Misson controllers accidentally confused inches and feet with metric units in calculating the spacecraft's course. This sent the orbiter on the wrong course, and it burned up in the Martian atmosphere.

MARS OBSERVER
The first of a series of NASA missions to study the geoscience and climate of Mars, Observer was launched in September 1992. Objectives included analysis of surface material and magnetic fields. Contact was lost in August 1993, three days before orbit was to begin. The spacecraft may still be in Mars orbit or is orbiting the Sun.

MARS POLAR LANDER
Launched by NASA on January 3, 1999, Mars Polar Lander carried two cylinders, seen at bottom. They were designed to penetrate the ground on impact. The mission was to find evidence of water ice and study the atmosphere. On December 3, 2000, the lander was about to descend when it went silent. Scientists desperately tried to reestablish contact, but its fate remains unknown.

Europe's Mars Express

THE EUROPEAN SPACE AGENCY (ESA) launched its first Mars mission in June 2003. Mars Express lifted off from Kazakhstan's Baikonur Cosmodrome on a Russian Soyuz/Fregat launcher. The spacecraft consisted of an orbiter and a lander. The lander, Beagle 2, had objectives that included high-resolution photography, mineralogical mapping, and study of the atmosphere. Beagle 2 was to study geology and geochemistry, and was equipped to look for evidence of past life. Unfortunately, soon after its release on December 19, Beagle 2 stopped sending signals. The lander was presumed lost, but the orbiter's advanced scientific instruments transmitted invaluable data. Mars Express Orbiter found evidence of water ice and past water activity.

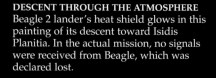

DESCENT THROUGH THE ATMOSPHERE
Beagle 2 lander's heat shield glows in this painting of its descent toward Isidis Planitia. In the actual mission, no signals were received from Beagle, which was declared lost.

EXPRESS AND BOOSTER
The Soyuz launch rocket has fallen away, and Mars Express is "parked" in orbit around the Earth. Next, the upper-stage Fregat booster rockets—at the bottom of the spacecraft—will fire to send Mars Express on its way to Mars.

SOYUZ GETS READY
The Soyuz launcher rocket is readied for liftoff at the Baikonur launch pad. Russian space technology was employed by ESA to propel Mars Express toward Mars. During its six-month journey, the spacecraft flew at a velocity of 6,710 mph (10,800 km/h).

IN ORBIT
Mars Express, at right, as it appears with the 130-foot (40 m) antennae booms unfurled. These antennae are for MARSIS (Mars Advanced Radar for Subsurface and Ionosphere Sounding) instruments, which can study the planet's crust as deep as 3 miles (5 km).

Extended antenna

IN SEARCH OF WATER
MARSIS radar waves penetrate the crust to analyze various types of material. The echoes that bounce back reveal information about the composition of the crust's top level. A prime objective is to find liquid water deep inside.

MARSIS antenna boom

Mars crust

Possible water reservoir

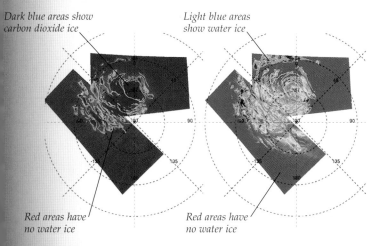

Dark blue areas show carbon dioxide ice

Light blue areas show water ice

Red areas have no water ice

Red areas have no water ice

OMEGA FINDS WATER ICE
In March 2004, the Mars Express OMEGA spectrometer showed carbon dioxide ice, far left, and water ice, near right, at the south polar region. Blue areas on the diagrams indicate a strong ice presence, while red shows lack of ice. All Mars Express instruments are programmed to look for the presence of water—liquid, vapor, or ice.

OMEGA'S VIEW
Three views of the South Polar region show, left, water ice; middle, carbon dioxide ice; and, right, the region as it appears to the eye.

Mars in three dimensions

Among the Mars Express mission's most spectacular results are the images transmitted by its High Resolution Stereo Color Camera (HRSC). This camera produces full-color, three-dimensional images of objects as small as 6.5 feet (2 m). Perhaps even the missing Beagle lander will one day be spotted by the HRSC.

Digital processing unit

Super-resolution optical system

High Resolution Stereo Color Camera

ALBOR THOLUS
The HRSC reveals wind-blown dust pouring into the caldera of Albor Tholus, a dormant Elysium volcano. Other Mars Express instruments detected the presence of methane gas on the planet. This is possible evidence of ongoing volcanism, which can produce methane.

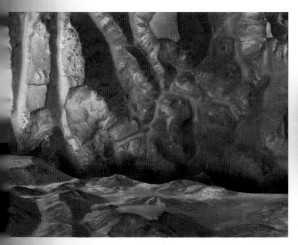

CRUISING OVER VALLES MARINERIS
Mars Express Orbiter's first stereoscopic color picture of Mars was taken by the HRSC in January 2004. A 1,056-mile (1,700 km) stretch of Valles Marineris is seen from 170 miles (275 km) above the surface.

WATER-SCULPTED FEATURES
Revealing photographs of dry riverbeds, sediments, and eroded features in eastern Valles Marineris are convincing proof that liquid water was abundant in the early history of the planet.

Martian mysteries

SCIENCE IS CONSTANTLY PROBING the many unknowns of Mars—the presence of liquid water, the question of ongoing volcanism, and whether there was or is life on the planet. Some centuries-old mysteries and myths have been answered. There is no intelligent life as we know it, no canals, no seas, no vegetation. Yet some images sent back by satellites have shown puzzling objects on Mars: clusters of pyramids, a sculptured dolphin, an ancient Egyptian queen, and a head with a crown. A few writers insisted these images showed artificial structures made by aliens long ago. Improved high-resolution cameras, however, have revealed that they are natural geological formations. It is the play of light and shadows on these formations that makes them appear like faces, animal forms, and man-made structures.

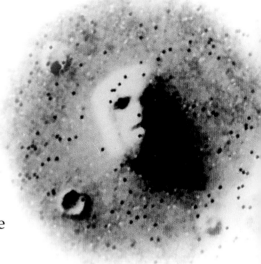

THE "FACE ON MARS"
There is an image among the buttes, knobs, and mesas near western Arabia Terra that is like a human face. Photographed by Viking 1 in 1976, it was considered the possible creation of intelligent beings. The "face" became the subject of talk shows, books, tabloids, and a movie. Then Mars Global Surveyor took a closer look.

GLOBAL SURVEYOR'S VIEW
In 2001, Global Surveyor's Mars Orbiter Camera made three-dimensional stereo images of the "face" from a distance of 280 miles (450 km). This possibly "artificial creation" showed itself as a natural mesa scarred by erosion. The feature is 2.2 miles (3.6 km) long and about .6 miles (1 km) wide. Sunlight illuminates the scene from the left.

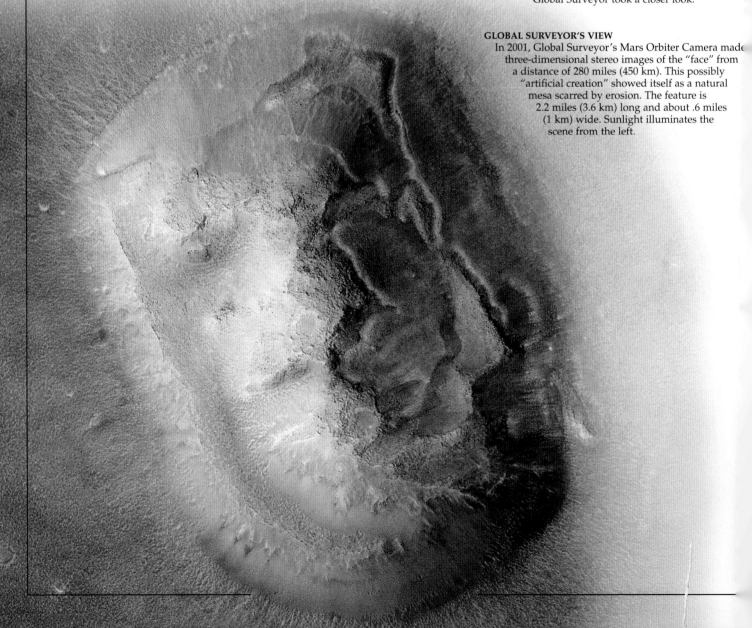

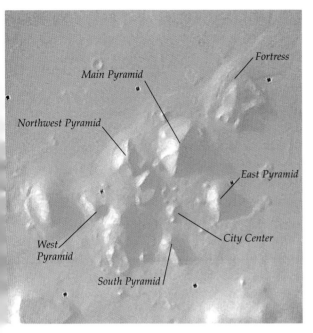

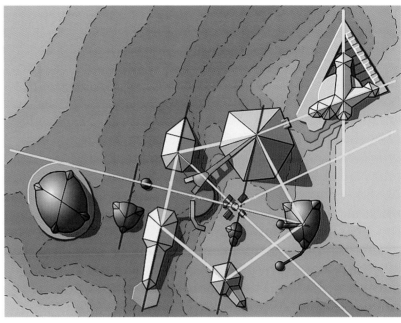

A LOST CITY OF PYRAMIDS
A few of the Viking orbiters' 1976 photographs of Martian landforms excited people who pursue mysteries. Some believed that this cluster of mesas and knobs in Cydonia near Acidalia Planitia are the ruined temples, forts, and pyramids of an ancient city. Shown in an image taken by a Viking orbiter, these features are matched in the diagram to the right.

ARTIST'S CONCEPTION OF A CYDONIAN "CITY"
The pyramidal forms in Cydonia are well known to those who pursue Martian "anomalies"—things that are unusual or abnormal. The architect who drew this interpretation linked the tops of five forms, making them corners of a pentagon. Some say this pentagonal layout of the features is the result of an intelligent plan, and that this is a long-abandoned city. The larger pyramidal forms are 1,000 times the size of the greatest ancient pyramids in Egypt.

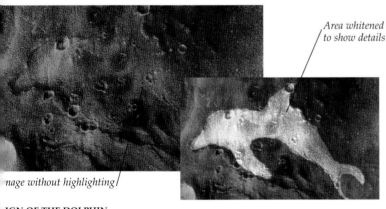

SIGN OF THE DOLPHIN
Similar to several man-made landforms on Earth, this dolphin-like formation from Cydonia becomes graphically clear when its photographic image is whitened. On Earth, such mysterious ancient forms appear designed to be seen by aircraft or space ships. On Mars, according to scientists, they are just natural formations.

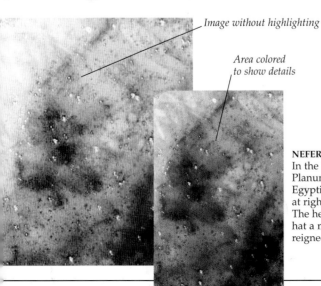

NEFERTITI ON MARS
In the Phoenicus Lacus region near Syria Planum the shadowy profile of a famous Egyptian queen can be seen. The photo at right is colored to show it more clearly. The head is 2,500 feet (750 m) across, the hat a mile (1.6 km) long. Nefertiti reigned in the 13th century BC.

HEAD WITH CROWN
Pictures such as this "Crowned Face," taken by Mars Global Surveyor, are closely studied by enthusiasts who look for unusual images. This feature, which is near Syrtis Major, is 11 miles (18 km) wide. Some viewers who look closely might find more than one "face" looking back.

Future exploration

IN COMING YEARS, a NASA Mars orbiter will release a small plane to make a low-level flight over the southern highlands. Plans are in the works for a group of European organizations and NASA to team up to launch the NetLander mission. In 2008, NASA's Phoenix lander will settle down on the North Polar region. The phoenix is a mythical bird that rises from the ashes—in this case from the 1999 loss of Mars Polar Lander. International space agencies are also discussing putting up a communications satellite, which their missions all could share. On drawing boards, too, are plans for possible manned flights to Mars and the establishment of permanent bases. NASA may use nuclear power for future Mars bases and rovers, which would give equipment a longer operating life than do solar arrays and batteries.

Video camera in tail

Sensors in wings

Spectrometers in nose

MARS AIRPLANE
This unmanned aircraft, named "Eagle," is part of a program known as ARES—Aerial Regional-scale Environment Survey of Mars. Ares is the Greek name for Mars. After release from an orbiter, the aircraft will fly at a height of nearly one mile (1.5 km), powered by a rocket engine. It will follow a 425-mile (680 km) course over the southern highlands as its science instruments send back data. Its wingspan is about 20 feet (6 m).

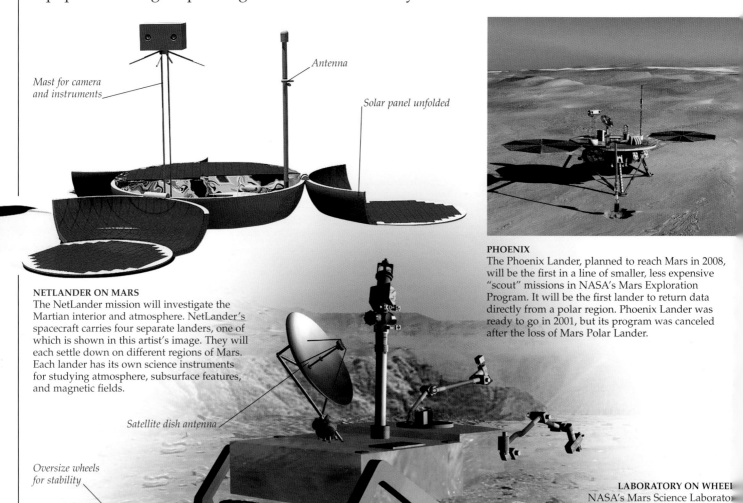

Mast for camera and instruments

Antenna

Solar panel unfolded

NETLANDER ON MARS
The NetLander mission will investigate the Martian interior and atmosphere. NetLander's spacecraft carries four separate landers, one of which is shown in this artist's image. They will each settle down on different regions of Mars. Each lander has its own science instruments for studying atmosphere, subsurface features, and magnetic fields.

Satellite dish antenna

Oversize wheels for stability

PHOENIX
The Phoenix Lander, planned to reach Mars in 2008, will be the first in a line of smaller, less expensive "scout" missions in NASA's Mars Exploration Program. It will be the first lander to return data directly from a polar region. Phoenix Lander was ready to go in 2001, but its program was canceled after the loss of Mars Polar Lander.

LABORATORY ON WHEEL
NASA's Mars Science Laborato
drives through a Martian canyo
in this artist's concept of a futu
rover. Scheduled for arrival
2010, the Mars Scien
Laboratory will analyze ro
and soil samples. NASA
considering nuclear energy f
powering the laboratory, whi
will be far more advanced tha
previous rove

Manned missions to Mars

Mars swings closest to Earth every two years, when a trip between the two planets requires 180 days. September 2007 offers the next opportunity to launch a manned program to Mars, but likely is too soon. NASA is considering the launching of three landers loaded with gear, supplies, and an astronaut return-vehicle. Two years later, two more supply landers would be sent. These would be followed two years after that by a spacecraft with a crew. Manned missions then could be sent every two years.

A BASE ON MARS
The transit module that carried the astronauts to Mars would serve as the crew's main quarters during their stay. Solar arrays would provide power, and astronauts could travel in large-sized rovers. Short-term stays would last 30–90 days, while long-term stays could be as long as 600 days.

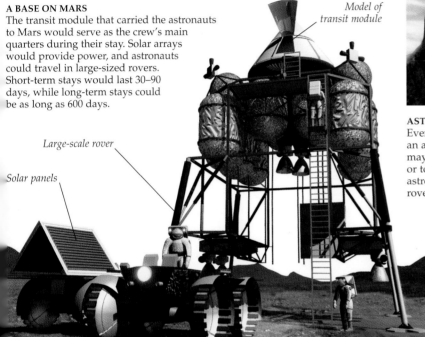

Model of transit module

Large-scale rover

Solar panels

ASTRONAUT GEOLOGISTS
Even the most sophisticated robotic rovers cannot go where an astronaut can. Future astronauts investigating Martian geology may rappel their way down cliff faces in search of specimens or to study rock formations up close. This artist's rendering shows astronauts scouting an outcrop, which they reached in a rover-type vehicle.

FUTURE SPACECRAFT
Laser-powered stations might one day propel spacecraft throughout the Solar System, as shown in this painting, which was created for NASA. The craft's dish antenna connects with a distant laser beam that provides energy. This spacecraft design is based on NASA studies, but since hardware and technology change rapidly, new space vessels will likely be different from the one pictured here.

Colonizing Mars

ONCE SPACE AGENCIES ARE ABLE to land spacecraft on Mars and relaunch them safely back to Earth, the next step would be manned missions. Astronaut pioneers would set up small outposts, living on supplies from Earth. They would work to build a safe "Planetary Surface Environment," as space scientists say. Colonization could follow, but permanent communities on Mars would need to be "biospheres"—places where plants can grow and fresh air is created. Researchers are developing large, airtight enclosures to serve as future biospheres on Mars. Some scientists go further and imagine planetary engineering to make Mars much like our Earth. Termed "terraforming," this would completely change the climate so that future human generations could live and breathe on Mars. Then they would be Martians.

MIRRORS MELT ICE
One concept for terraforming Mars is to put giant mirrors into orbit. They could reflect sunlight onto the planet's surface and melt water ice and carbon dioxide ice. The mirror cluster pictured here is warming up the South Polar region. This process would free gases and vapor in order to thicken and improve the atmosphere.

ON TO MARS!
This "adventure-travel" poster was created by enthusiasts who dream of riding a "Mars Express" tourist spacecraft. On Mars, they would explore volcanoes, live in luxurious greenhouses, prospect for asteroids, and even make expeditions to the outer planets.

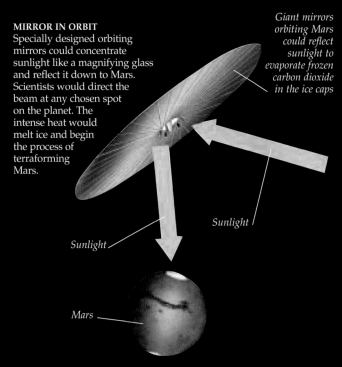

MIRROR IN ORBIT
Specially designed orbiting mirrors could concentrate sunlight like a magnifying glass and reflect it down to Mars. Scientists would direct the beam at any chosen spot on the planet. The intense heat would melt ice and begin the process of terraforming Mars.

Giant mirrors orbiting Mars could reflect sunlight to evaporate frozen carbon dioxide in the ice caps

Sunlight

Sunlight

Mars

ENGINEERED CLIMATE CHANGE
Three stages of terraforming are shown in these paintings, starting with a desert. The second stage is a cold, watery environment with a blue sky, indicating denser air. In the third stage, there are green meadows, trees, and ponds. The atmosphere is thick enough to fill the sky with clouds.

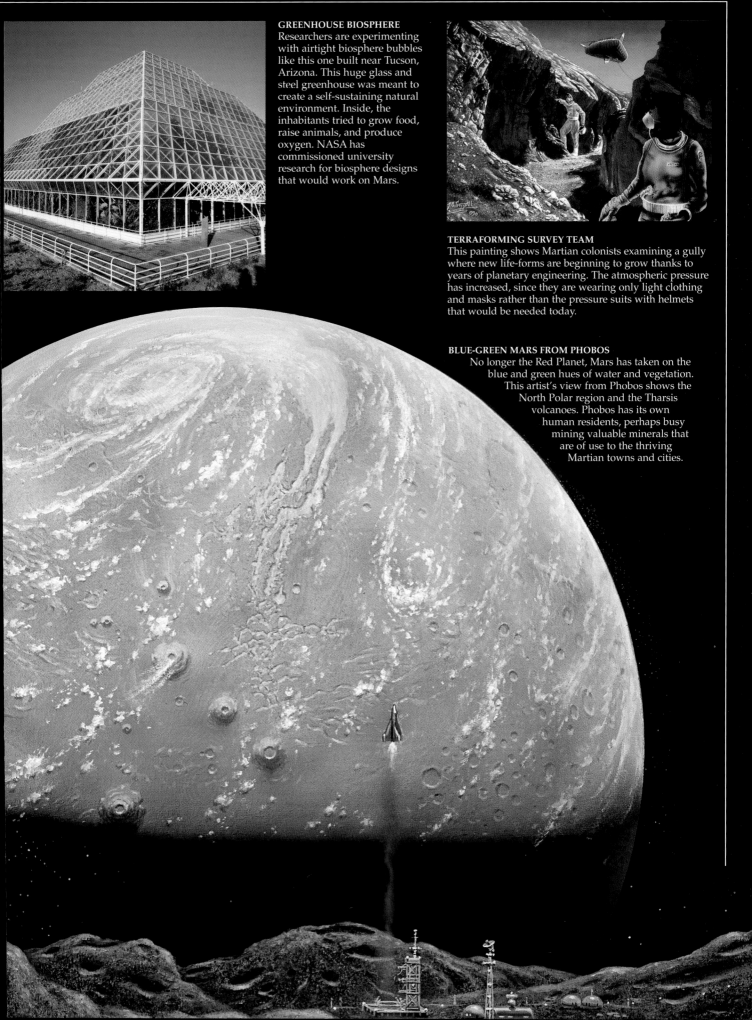

GREENHOUSE BIOSPHERE
Researchers are experimenting with airtight biosphere bubbles like this one built near Tucson, Arizona. This huge glass and steel greenhouse was meant to create a self-sustaining natural environment. Inside, the inhabitants tried to grow food, raise animals, and produce oxygen. NASA has commissioned university research for biosphere designs that would work on Mars.

TERRAFORMING SURVEY TEAM
This painting shows Martian colonists examining a gully where new life-forms are beginning to grow thanks to years of planetary engineering. The atmospheric pressure has increased, since they are wearing only light clothing and masks rather than the pressure suits with helmets that would be needed today.

BLUE-GREEN MARS FROM PHOBOS
No longer the Red Planet, Mars has taken on the blue and green hues of water and vegetation. This artist's view from Phobos shows the North Polar region and the Tharsis volcanoes. Phobos has its own human residents, perhaps busy mining valuable minerals that are of use to the thriving Martian towns and cities.

Did you know?

FASCINATING FACTS

The great Babylonian astronomers and mathematicians of 2000–1600 BC accurately calculated the positions and movements of the stars and planets. Some of their calculations were preserved on tablets made of clay that hardened and were preserved as long-lasting records.

A Babylonian clay tablet with an algebraic-geometrical calculation

Mars is often the third brightest object in our night sky after the Moon and the planet Venus. At other times, the orbit of Mars takes it so far away that it is much dimmer, like a star.

Viking god Tiu with a bear on a 6th-century plaque

The Vikings of northern Europe worshipped their own fierce god of war. Called Tiu, Vikings honored him by using his name for a day of the week: Tuesday.

Seen from the Martian surface, the larger moon, Phobos, is only one-twentieth as bright as our own Moon appears to us. The smaller Martian moon, Deimos, is like a star.

Although Mars is little more than half the size of Earth, the Red Planet has the same total land area as Earth. This is because most of Earth's surface is covered with water, while Mars is dry.

Martian winds are much less powerful than winds on Earth because the atmosphere on Mars is so thin. This causes even the strongest winds on Mars, about 80 mph (133 km), to have little force. Winds are usually light, around 6 miles (3.75 km) an hour.

Many of the large craters on Mars are named for famous scientists, such as Copernicus, Herschel, Huygens, Kepler, Galileo Galilei, and Isaac Newton. Later astronomers honored with large craters include Schiaparelli and Lowell. Many other people have craters named after them including Orson Welles, producer of the famous "War of the Worlds" radio broadcast.

The sunlight reflected by the Earth, as seen from the surface of Mars, is called "Earthshine."

Phobos and Deimos might be remnants of a larger moon that broke up many millions of years ago. This may have happened when the moon's orbit brought it too close to the planet and the pull of gravity caused it to shatter.

There are places on Mars where radar signals strike the surface and vanish. This is because Martian dust is too thick for signals to get through. Landers avoid these places because they use radar signals to indicate the distance to the ground when they descend.

Chesley Bonestell's painting of snowdrifts in a polar region

So much water ice exists in Martian polar regions that scientists believe it would flood the planet if it melted.

A painting of a Martian moon shattering

QUESTIONS AND ANSWERS

Q Do the two Martian moons orbit in the same direction?

A Yes, but it does not look that way from Mars. Phobos and Deimos seem to go in opposite directions. Phobos orbits the planet three times for every revolution of Mars—a Martian day. Seen from Mars, Phobos rises in the West and sets in the East. Deimos takes three days to complete an orbit, rising in the East and setting in the West.

Q How often do Mars and Earth come nearest to each other?

A On August 27, 2003, Mars made its closest approach to Earth in nearly 60,000 years. The distance between the planets then was approximately 34.6 million miles (55.7 million km). The last time Mars came so close was in 57,617 BC!

Q Who named Olympus Mons?

A Italian astronomer Giovanni Schiaparelli gave this shield volcano the name Nix Olympicus—the "Snows of Olympus." It appeared in his telescope as a white area in the orange Martian surface. Schiaparelli named it after Mount Olympus, mythical home of the Greek gods. In 1971, images from Mariner 9 showed it was a volcano, and NASA scientists renamed it Olympus Mons—Mount Olympus.

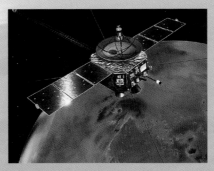

Japanese orbiter, Nozomi

Q Have only the U.S. and European space programs sent spacecraft close to Mars in recent years?

A No, NASA and the European Space Agency are now joined by the Japanese space program. The Japanese launched Nozomi in 1998, but the spacecraft ran low on fuel. Unable to complete its objectives, Nozomi passed within 625 miles (1,000 km) of Mars and kept going. The craft was reprogrammed to orbit the Sun.

Q Did Mars ever have much water?

A There is evidence that Mars had liquid water, water ice, and water vapor until 3.9 billion years ago. One source of vapor could have been hot springs—vents in the Martian surface.

Q Why search for information about past Martian weather?

A Understanding the past climate of Mars could help scientists discover whether the planet supported life. Part of the mission of NASA's Mars Climate Orbiter, launched in 1998, was to look for clues about past Martian climates and how they changed. The spacecraft unfortunately crashed on its approach.

Climate Orbiter being tested

Illustration of a hot spring on early Mars

Mars Mosts

 MOST AIMED-AT PLANET
By 2004, 37 missions had been launched at Mars, mostly by the U.S. and the former Soviet Union. Venus is the second most-targeted planet, with 25 launches.

 MOST LIKE EARTH
The Martian day, 24 hours and 39 minutes, is about the same as Earth's 23 hours and 56 minutes; both planets spin on axes with similar tilts—Earth at 23.4 degrees, Mars at 25.2 degrees; and this tilt gives each planet changing seasons as they orbit the Sun.

 MARS: HIGHEST AND DEEPEST
The Solar System's highest mountain is Olympus Mons, 84,500 feet (25 km); its deepest canyon is Valles Marineris, 4 miles (7 km).

 CLOSEST MOON
Of the 137 moons in the Solar System, the one with the closest orbit is Phobos, the larger of the two Martian satellites.

 THE REDDEST PLANET
Mars is orange-red because a large amount of oxidized iron is in the soil. Oxidized iron can be brown, yellow, orange, or red.

Timeline

Wise men of ancient days observed the heavens and gave meaning and names to what they saw. They passed on their knowledge to philosopher-scientists such as Aristotle and Ptolemy. The works of these men, in turn, were studied by Copernicus and others who developed new ideas. Next, telescopes brought the stars and planets closer, and scientists searched Mars for signs of life. Popular culture turned scientific theory into stories of high adventure, inspiring young people to become astronomers and learn more about their universe, Solar System, and Mars. Science fiction became reality in the 1960s, when an American probe was the first spacecraft to visit the Red Planet.

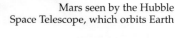

Mars seen by the Hubble Space Telescope, which orbits Earth

2000 BC–300 BC ANCIENTS
Egyptians call the "wandering star" *Har Décher*, "The Red One." Later peoples observe the planet the Romans come to call Mars, after their god of war.

4TH–1ST CENTURIES BC
Aristotle studies Mars and considers the cosmos. Hipparchus charts hundreds of stars and several planets.

100–200 AD GEOCENTRISM
Ptolemy teaches geocentrism—that the planets and Sun revolve around Earth.

1500–1600 HELIOCENTRISM
Copernicus breaks with geocentrism, influencing later astronomers to accept heliocentrism, a Sun-centered system.

Angelo Secchi

1600–1750 MEASURING MARS
Italian astronomer Galileo Galilei (1564–1642) is first to observe Mars through a telescope. Huygens improves telescope design, and believes there could be life on Mars. Astronomers make ever-more precise measurements of Mars.

1726 THE MARTIAN MOONS
In his satirical novel, *Gulliver's Travels*, Swift describes Mars as having two moons.

1780s HERSCHEL STUDIES MARS
Herschel calculates inclination of Mars's axis of rotation to be approximately 24 degrees; suggests the planet could support life.

1858 SECCHI'S CANALE
Italian astronomer Angelo Secchi (1818–1878) renames Huygens's "Hourglass Sea" as "Atlantic Canale," using the term canal or channel in relation to Mars for the first time.

1877 DISCOVERING THE MOONS
Hall observes two tiny moons orbiting Mars. He names them Phobos and Deimos.

1877–1878 NAMES AND CANALS
Schiaparelli calls geometric patterns on Mars "canali" meaning "channels." His description is misinterpreted as meaning artificially made canals. He gives names to much of what he sees.

1880s POPULAR IDEA
The belief that Mars is inhabited becomes the conventional wisdom.

1892 COMPILING OBSERVATIONS
The Planet Mars by French astronomer Camille Flammarion (1842–1925) collects all observations from 1600s to 1892.

1894–1895 CANALS AND VEGETATION
Lowell builds Arizona observatory and publishes his theory that Mars has canals, liquid water, and vegetation. This is contradicted by Barnard shortly thereafter.

1896 MARTIAN BEINGS
H. G. Wells writes article, "Intelligence on Mars"; believes Martian life has developed parallel to life on Earth.

1897 INTERPLANETARY WARFARE
Martian landings on Earth are popular subjects for authors, and Wells's novel *War of the Worlds* becomes hugely popular.

Engraving from *War of the Worlds*

1907 NEW CANAL THEORY
English scientist Alfred Wallace (1823–1913) explains Martian canals as natural features.

1912 BURROUGHS ON MARS
Mars adventure, "Under the Moons of Mars," starts Burroughs writing Mars stories. With Wells and Lowell, he influences future Mars fiction, radio shows, and film.

1938 TERROR IN A RADIO-PLAY
Radio drama of *War of the Worlds* causes panic in New Jersey.

Percival Lowell

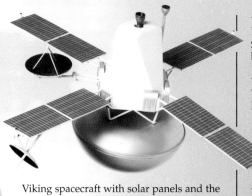

Viking spacecraft with solar panels and the metal capsule which contains the lander

1960 MARSNIK FAILS
Soviet Union launches the probe Marsnik 1 to fly by Mars. It is the first of eight unsuccessful Soviet attempts to reach Mars in the 1960s.

1964 MARINER 4 SUCCEEDS
U.S. launches Mariner 3 to fly by Mars, but it fails. Mariner 4 becomes the first spacecraft to fly by Mars, which is shown to be dry and pocked by craters.

1969 MARINERS FLY BY
Mariners 6 and 7 launch and fly successfully past Mars.

1971 FIRST TO ORBIT
Mariner 8 fails, but Mariner 9 becomes the first American spacecraft to orbit another planet.

Illustration of the Mars Exploration Rover

1971–1974 SOVIET DISAPPOINTMENTS
Soviets launch seven more Mars missions, but none is fully successful.

1976 VIKING LANDERS
Viking 1 makes the first successful Mars landing, followed by Viking 2.

1988 MORE DISAPPOINTMENTS
The Soviets' Phobos 1 and 2 fail to operate properly.

1992 U.S.'S OBSERVER FAILS
U.S.'s Mars Observer is lost.

1996 SURVEYOR AND PATHFINDER
U.S. launches Global Surveyor. Russia's Mars 96 orbiter and lander fails. U.S. launches Pathfinder, carrying the first rover.

1997 UNMATCHED SUCCESS
Pathfinder lands on Mars, and Global Surveyor goes into orbit, both triumphs.

1998 JAPAN SENDS FIRST MISSION
Japanese launch Nozomi, but the mission fails. U.S.'s Mars Climate Orbiter also fails.

1999 ANOTHER FAILURE
U.S.'s Mars Polar Lander fails.

2001 ODYSSEY MAPS MARS
U.S. launches 2001 Mars Odyssey, which orbits and maps the planet.

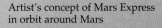

Artist's concept of Mars Express in orbit around Mars

2003 EXPLORATION ROVERS
U.S. launches two Mars Exploration Rover spacecraft. On August 27, at 9:46 a.m. GMT, Mars and Earth are the nearest in 59,619 years—34.6 million miles (55.8 million km) apart. The European Space Agency launches Mars Express, which carries a lander.

2004 TRIUMPH AND LOSS
The Mars Exploration Rovers are successful. Mars Express lander is lost, although orbiter

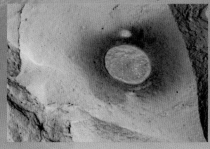

Mars rock named "Humphrey," with a hole drilled by Spirit Rover

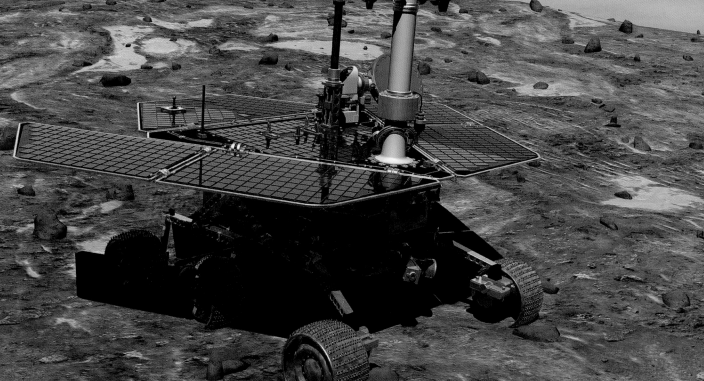

Find out more

OUR KNOWLEDGE OF MARS is increasing almost as fast as public interest in the Red Planet is growing. Museums, observatories, planetariums, websites, and our schools make discovering Mars an exciting and ever-changing experience. Whether through a telescope or in a museum, the possibilities are all around us for taking an up-close look at Mars and its missions, images, spacecraft, robots, technology, and scientists.

NATIONAL AIR AND SPACE MUSEUM
The Space Race Gallery at the National Air and Space Museum (NASM) in Washington, D.C., exhibits rockets used both by the military and for exploring space. Rockets designed to carry bombs also have been used to send spacecraft and astronauts into space. The history of space exploration is on display at NASM, part of the Smithsonian Institution. NASM has the world's largest collection of historic spacecraft.

THE PALOMAR OBSERVATORY
The Palomar Observatory in San Diego County, California, is open daily to the public during daytime hours. Visitors can take self-guided tours to the 200-inch Hale Telescope in the revolving dome. At night scientists have the observatory to themselves to conduct research using telescopes of various sizes and the Palomar All-Sky Camera. Palomar is owned and operated by the California Institute of Technology.

Places to Visit

SMITHSONIAN NATIONAL AIR AND
SPACE MUSEUM (2 locations)
    National Mall
    6th & Independence Avenue, SW
    Washington, DC 20560

    14390 Air and Space Museum Pkwy
    Chantilly, VA 20151

PALOMAR OBSERVATORY
35899 Canfield Road
Palomar Mountain, CA 92060-0200

HAYDEN PLANETARIUM
American Museum of Natural History
Central Park West at 79th Street
New York, NY 10024-5192

CHABOT SPACE AND SCIENCE CENTER
10000 Skyline Boulevard
Oakland, CA 94619

JET PROPULSION LABORATORY
4800 Oak Grove Drive
Pasadena, California 91109

HAYDEN PLANETARIUM
Viewers lift off into interplanetary space when they visit the Space Theater in New York City's Hayden Planetarium. The Space Theater is in the huge Hayden Sphere, pictured here. The theater has the largest and most powerful virtual-reality simulator in the world. The Planetarium is part of the American Museum of Natural History's Rose Center for Earth and Space, which offers programs and exhibits on Mars missions.

WATCHING MARS

THE BEST TIME TO VIEW the Red Planet is at opposition, when Mars and the Earth are nearest. This happens every two years—2005, 2007, etc.—during August or September. A moderately good telescope can see the white polar caps in the north and south. The darker areas of the surface may look greenish. This is caused by the contrast in color between the dark patches and the redder, brighter areas. The best views of all are every 15 or 17 years, when the closest opposition occurs.

THE FAMILY TELESCOPE
This mirror-lens telescope with a computer-controlled, battery-powered motor drive is a bit complicated for children to operate by themselves, so an adult is present. Mars is a favorite observation target for backyard astronomers. It is the only planet where the average astronomer can observe the seasons change. Moderately sized telescopes can see the polar ice caps grow bigger in winter and become smaller in summer.

MARS THROUGH 3-D GLASSES
Scientists at NASA's Jet Propulsion Laboratory in California wear special glasses to view three-dimensional images transmitted to Earth from the Mars Exploration Rover mission. Below is a 3-D version of the Rover Opportunity's view of Eagle Crater. Rover tracks are visible in the Martian dust at right. This image, taken by the rover's navigation camera, overlooks the lander's deployed petals.

Glossary

AMAZONIAN AGE The most recent Martian historical period, beginning about 2.5 billion years ago and continuing until today.

ASH Fine-grained material produced by a volcanic eruption and thrown into the atmosphere in a cloud.

ASTEROID Any of the small celestial bodies with orbits between Mars and Jupiter.

ASTRONOMY Generally, the study of the planets and stars, and the laws that govern their movements.

Olympus Mons caldera

BIOSPHERE A natural system that contains all the elements required for life, including rain and warmth and the capacity for producing air that can be breathed.

CALDERA A large depression at the top of a volcano. Volcanic calderas are produced by the collapse of a magma chamber or by an explosive eruption that removes the upper part of the volcano.

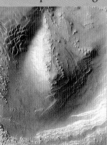

CHASMA A gash in the land's surface, often a deep canyon.

CONE The peak of a volcano, formed by lava pouring down the sides and cooling into steep slopes.

Ganges Chasma

CORE The center of a planet; the cores of Earth and Mars are mostly iron.

CRATER A depression, usually with a rim, formed by the impact of a meteorite. Also, a depression around the opening or vent of a volcano.

CRUST The outer layer of a planet, above the mantle and core.

DUST DEVIL A twisting updraft of wind that raises dust and soil into a small cyclone and moves across the ground.

EJECTA Material, such as mud or fragmented rock, that is thrown out of an impact crater during its formation.

ELLIPSE The egg-shaped orbit of a planet, moon, or a man-made satellite. The orbits of the planets are ellipses, not circles.

EROSION The wearing away of soil or rock as a result of the action of wind and water.

EXPLOSIVE ERUPTION A violent volcanic eruption that throws debris high into the air. The resulting fast-flowing lava often builds up a steep cone.

FLYBY The flight of a spacecraft, generally termed a probe, which passes a planet without attempting to land or to orbit.

GEOCENTRIC Earth-centered: the theory that the Earth is the center of the Solar System, and the planets and Sun revolve around the Earth.

HELIOCENTRIC Sun-centered: the theory that the Sun is the center of the Solar System, and the planets revolve around it.

HESPERIAN AGE The middle period in Martian history, beginning about 3.5 billion years ago and lasting until about 2.5 billion years ago.

HOT SPOT A point on a planet's surface that is warmer than its surroundings and could be heat from a rising plume in the planet's mantle.

ICE TOWERS Frozen formations created by the venting of steam from under the Antarctic surface ice; inside temperatures are warmer than the outside air.

IMPACT CRATER A basinlike depression caused by the crash of an object falling from space; usually surrounded by a rim and by ejecta that lands all around.

JOVIAN PLANET Any one of the four gaseous outer planets: Jupiter, Saturn, Uranus, and Neptune.

LABYRINTHUS An intersecting network of valleys.

LANDER Part of a spacecraft that detaches and lands on a planet.

LAVA Molten rock that flows from underground onto the surface.

LIMB The outer edge, or horizon, of a celestial body, usually as viewed from above the surface.

MAGMA Molten rock within the crust of a planet that can push through to the surface and become lava.

MANTLE The area inside a planet, below the crust and surrounding the core.

METEOR The glow seen when a meteoroid burns in the atmosphere, often termed a shooting star.

METEORITE The part of a meteoroid that survives the fall through a planet's atmosphere and strikes the surface.

METEOROID A small rock in space.

MONS A mountain, often a volcano.

NOACHIAN The first Martian historical period, beginning about 4.5 billion years ago and lasting until about 3.5 billion years ago.

OPPOSITION The relationship when a celestial body passes between another body and the Sun. The Earth and Mars are in opposition when Earth passes between Mars and the Sun, placing Mars on the opposite side of the Earth from the Sun.

Painting of Noctis Labyrinthus

ORBIT The path of a body that is moving around a second body or a point.

ORBITER A spacecraft that orbits a planet.

PATERA A shallow crater, often also a volcano.

PLANITIA Broad lowlands plains.

PLANUM A plateau or high plain.

POLAR HOOD The shroud of clouds that forms over the Martian Northern Polar region in wintertime.

PROBE A spacecraft with a mission to approach a planet but not to land, orbit, or return to Earth.

RAMPART CRATER A crater surrounded by sloping ejecta blankets, usually formed by the impact throwing up and melting underground ice; the ice flies out of the crater and creates rampart-like masses around the rim.

REVOLUTION The movement of a planet around the Sun, or of a moon around a planet.

ROTATION The spinning of a planet. One full rotation is a day.

ROVER A robotic machine that travels over the surface of a planet and conducts experiments, or that could transport astronauts from place to place on a planet.

SATELLITE A body that revolves around a larger body; a man-made spacecraft in orbit.

Above Olympus Mons

SHIELD VOLCANO A volcano in the shape of a flattened dome and with gradual slopes; formed by underground pressure that lifts the surface and by lava flows.

SECONDARY IMPACT CRATERS Additional craters formed by the fall of ejecta debris during the creation of an impact crater.

SOLAR SYSTEM A sun and all the bodies that revolve around it.

SPECTROMETERS Scientific instruments that estimate the absorption and emission of light and other radiation; by studying the spectrometer's data, scientists can tell what minerals and chemicals are in a planet's rock and soil.

Hellas Planitia

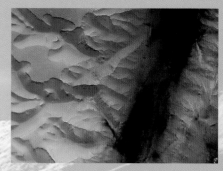

Louros Valles

SPECTROSCOPY The study of how various materials reflect or radiate light as measured by spectrometers.

SURFACE MICROROVER A small robotic machine that can travel over a planet's surface to conduct scientific experiments.

TERRAFORMING The process of changing a planet's climate in order to make it more habitable, and more like Earth.

THOLUS A small-domed mountain or hill, often a volcano.

VALLIS A valley, often winding.

VASTITAS A vast lowland.

VENT The opening in a planet's crust through which volcanic material erupts.

VOLCANO A vent in the planetary surface through which lava, gases, and ash erupt.

WANDERING STARS An ancient name for the planets, which seem to move across the heavens while the "fixed" stars keep the same relative positions in the night sky.

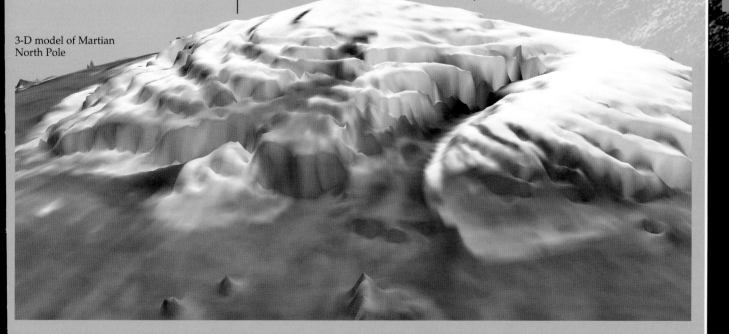

3-D model of Martian North Pole

Index

Acknowledgments

Media Projects, Inc. and DK Publishing, Inc., offer grateful thanks to: Tony Reichhardt of *Smithsonian Air & Space Magazine;* Dr. Robert H. van Ghent of the Institute of Mathematics and Natural Sciences in Utrecht, The Netherlands; Ron Miller; Kees Veenenbos; Dr. William K. Hartmann and Kathleen Komarek of the Planetary Science Institute, Tucson, Arizona; and Jennifer Seitz of NASA.

Photography and Art Credits
(t=top; b=bottom; l=left; r=right; c=center; a=above)
Bantam Books, a division of Random House, Inc.: 10tr. **British Astronomical Association, Mars Section:** 12tr. **James Burmester:** 17c, 18tr, 22tr, 27c, 30br, 40c, 41t, 46bl. **Ben Bussey:** 49bl. **Courtesy of the Archives, California Institute of Technology:** 12bl. **California Space Institute:** 49cr, 49bl, 55tl. **Stanimir Metchev/Caltech Department of Astronomy:** 12br. **Michael Carroll Art:** 63tr; Michael Carroll/Space Science Institute: 36cr. © **CORBIS:** 8ca, 66b; © Alinari Archives/CORBIS: 7bl; © Paul Almasy/CORBIS: 8tr; © Richard Berenholtz/CORBIS: 68b; © James P. Blair/CORBIS: 68tl; © Geoffrey Clements/CORBIS: 7ca; © Werner Forman/CORBIS: 64bl; © ROBERT GALBRAITH/Reuters/Corbis: 69cr;

© Hulton-Deutsch Collection/CORBIS: 8cb, 10cl; © David Lees/CORBIS: 64cl; © Gianni Dagli Orti/CORBIS: 7tl; © Gabe Palmer/CORBIS: 69cl; © Enzo & Paolo Ragazzini/CORBIS: 6b; © NASA/Roger Ressmeyer/CORBIS: 23cr; © Bill Ross/CORBIS: 68c; © Joseph Sohm, ChromoSohm Inc./CORBIS: 63tl; © CORBIS SYGMA: 11cl; © Underwood & Underwood/CORBIS: 11tr, 11cr. **Brian Duval, courtesy Lynn Rothschild:** 4cr, 50cb. *A Princess of Mars* cover art courtesy of **Edgar Rice Burroughs, Inc.** Trademarks John Carter of Mars TM and Barsoom TM Owned by Edgar Rice Burroughs, Inc. and Used by Permission: 11tll. **Copyright ESA:** 54br, 56cl, 56cr, 56bl, 56br, 57 All, 70tl, 71tr; ESA 2001, Illustration by Medialab: 24tl, 56tr; ESA-D. Ducros: 67tr; ESA/DLR/FU Berlin (G. Neukum): 40tl, 50bl. **Eugène Antoniadi, la planète Mars:** 12tc. **Ken Fair/Electricolive.com:** 62tl. **Robert Fiertek:** 59tr. **Martyn Fogg:** 62cl. **Courtesy Calvin J. Hamilton** www.solarviews.com: 14c, 25tcl, 25tc, 25tr, 41cr, 41clb, 41bl, 41bc, 41br, 45cl. © **David A. Hardy**/www.astroart.org, from FUTURES by David A Hardy & Patrick Moore: 63b Paintings © **Dr. William K. Hartmann, Planetary Science Institute, Tucson, A.Z.:** 23t, 35br, 36b, 38tl, 43tr. **Photograph courtesy Dr. William K. Hartmann, Planetary Science Institute, Tucson, A.Z.:** 25cl. Copyright 1998 **ISAS. Create by Yasushi YOSHIDA:** 55tr, 65t.

Adrian Lark, www.mars3d.com: 4clb, 33tra, 33trb, 33c. David Lauterbach, **www.lightworld.net:** 62b. Los Alamos **National Laboratory:** 47tl. Courtesy of the **Lowell Observatory:** 9bl, 9cr. **Lunar and Planetary Institute:** 34bl. Photo courtesy of Lunar Planetary Library: 12ca, 45cr. **Teemu Mäkinen/Finnish Meteorological Institute:** 60cl. **Courtesy Marilynn Flynn:** 25br, 27br. Walter Meyers, www.arcadiastreet.com/cgvistas: 26b. **Courtesy Ron Miller,** copyright Bonestell Space Art: 13cl, 13b, 66cr. **Paintings by Ron Miller:** 4bl, 11b, 41cl, 42b, 44b, 46cr, 51b, 52t, 64br, 65bl, 70br. **Photograph courtesy Ron Miller:** 51tr. **Mount Erebus Volcano Observatory, N.M. Tech.:** 51cl. **Musée de l'air et de l'espace:** 13tr. **NASA:** 9t, 18cl, 18bl, 19tl, 19tr, 19c, 19br, 25cr, 28cr, 29tr, 35t, 37c, 45tl, 46cl, 49cl, 60cr, 61tr, 61b, 66 background, 69b, 71tl, 71c; NASA GSFC: 14c, 14cb, 14br, 15bl, 15br, 35ca, 55c, 66tr, 71b; NASA JPL: 2tc, 2tr, 4br, 14tl, 15tr, 20tl, 20cl, 20lb, 20b, 23c,28t, 28cl, 28b, 29c, 31c, 31b, 31br, 32, 33b, 47, 48tl, 49cr, 51ct, 55br, 60b, 65cr, 67cr, 70cl; NASA/JPL/Cornell: 52b, 53 All; Dan Maas, NASA JPL: 1, 52c, 67b; NASA/JPL/Malin Space Science Systems: 2cl, 4tr, 27cl, 34cl, 35cb, 35cr, 39tr, 39cla, 39cl, 39ca, 39c, 42tc, 42c, 42cr, 43tl, 43c, 45tr, 46br, 50ca, 50tr, 58tr, 58b, 59l, 59cr; NASA Kennedy Space Center: 14bl, 30bl; NASA /Langley Research Center: 5t, 60t; Nasa/Marshall Space Flight Center: 13tl;

MSSS/JPL/NASA Artwork by JP Levasseur: 59bl; MSSS/JPL/NASA Taken from Metaresearch.org: 59cl; National Space Science Data Center/NASA: 4tl, 54tr, 54bl, 61c. **National Oceanic and Atmospheric Administration/Department of Commerce:** 4lca, 25bl. © A. Tayfun Oner: 26lb, 26la **Sahara Met:** 49tl; Photograph by R. Pelisson, SaharaMet: 49tr. **Science Photo Library:** 8br. **Don Davis for SETI Institute:** 48b. **University of California/Lick Observatory:** 9br. **Courtesy USGS:** 37tr; USGS/Photo Researchers, Inc.: 16bl. **Geoff Chester, courtesy U.S. Naval Observatory Library:** 27tl, 27tcl, 27tr. **Kees Veenenbos** www.space4case.com The Netherlands; data: **The MOLA science team:** 3, 22b, 24b, 34cr, 37tl, 37br, 39b, 40b, 44tr, 64–65 background, 68–69 background, 70–71 background; Kees Veenenbos/NASA: 2c, 22c, 46tl.

Cover Credits:
Julian Baum: cover tr. **Ben Bussey:** back cover bc. **California Space Institute:** cover tl. © **CORBIS:** back cover tl. **Adrian Lark,** www.mars3d.com: back cover tr. **Courtesy of the Lowell Observatory:** back cover bl. **Painting by Ron Miller:** back cover cr. **Nasa JPL:** Cover tla, back cover c; NASA / SCIENCE PHOTO LIBRARY: cover ca. **National Oceanic and Atmospheric Administration/Department of Commerce:** back cover br.